GATHER

GATHER

RICHARD VAN CAMP

ON THE JOY OF STORYTELLING

 University of Regina Press

Printed and bound in Canada at Imprimerie Gauvin. The text of this book is printed on 100% post-consumer recycled paper with earth-friendly vegetable-based inks.

Cover and text design: Duncan Campbell, University of Regina Press
Copy editor: Rhonda Kronyk
Proofreader: Rachel Taylor
Cover art: "Campfire in the Wilderness with the Northern Lights" by iStockPhoto/ solarseven.

Library and Archives Canada Cataloguing in Publication

TITLE: Gather : Richard Van Camp on the joy of storytelling.

NAMES: Van Camp, Richard, author.

SERIES: Writers on writing (Regina, Sask.) ; 3.

DESCRIPTION: Series statement: Writers on writing ; 3 | Includes bibliographical references.

IDENTIFIERS: Canadiana (print) 2021011942X | Canadiana (ebook) 20210119446 | ISBN 9780889778047 (hardcover) | ISBN 9780889777002 (softcover) | ISBN 9780889777026 (PDF) | ISBN 9780889777040 (EPUB)

SUBJECTS: LCSH: Storytelling. | LCSH: Folklore—Performance. | LCSH: Storytelling—Technique. | LCSH: Storytelling—Psychological aspects.

CLASSIFICATION: LCC GR72.3 .V36 2021 | DDC 808.5/43—dc23

10 9 8 7 6 5 4 3 2 1

University of Regina Press, University of Regina
Regina, Saskatchewan, Canada, S4S 0A2
TEL: (306) 585-4758 FAX: (306) 585-4699
WEB: www.uofrpress.ca

We acknowledge the support of the Canada Council for the Arts for our publishing program. We acknowledge the financial support of the Government of Canada. / Nous reconnaissons l'appui financier du gouvernement du Canada. This publication was made possible with support from Creative Saskatchewan's Book Publishing Production Grant Program.

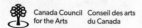 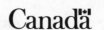

*For our storytellers past, present and future, and for
everyone that you're about to meet in* Gather.

*Bless you and the soul medicine that you
weave. Your words have guided my life.*

*For my wife, Keavy, and our son, Edzazü.
I love you with all I have and more.*

*I am grateful to every storyteller who I have mentioned in this
celebration of family and community. You braid stories and
hope together to blanket your listeners with peace and hope.
I am grateful. We are grateful. Mahsi cho.*

WRITERS ON WRITING

The Writers on Writing series offers readers witty, conversational reflections on a wide range of craft-related topics, as well as practical advice for writers and the writing life at any level. The books are accessible and handy, yet they don't shy away from the challenges of writing. They'll become your friends. Think of sitting down in a coffee shop in conversation with a smart, friendly, veteran author. Part inspiration, part advice, part anecdote—total oxygen after all those stuffy writing textbooks.

Jeanette Lynes, Series Editor

FOR MORE INFORMATION ON THE
Writers on Writing SERIES, CONTACT:

University of Regina Press
3737 Wascana Parkway
Regina, SK S4S 0A2
uofrpress@uregina.ca
www.uofrpress.ca

PREVIOUS BOOKS IN THE
Writers on Writing SERIES:

Sleuth: Gail Bowen on Writing Mysteries,
by Gail Bowen (2018)

Voice: Adam Pottle on Writing with Deafness
by Adam Pottle (2019)

CONTENTS

May your home be so holy with laughter
that wounded birds lean against
your door to listen and heal.
—MY TWITTER AND FACEBOOK POSTS,
JULY 22, 2017

HELLO! I'VE MISSED YOU

Edanet'e? Hello! How are you, Cousin? I've missed you. Talk about living through hard times of late, hey, with the pandemic and all the uncertainty in the world? But we've learned a lot, too, in this major moment that we have called COVID-19, haven't we, despite losses and fears and the lockdowns and the unknowns? We've learned that we need each other, we need to reset, we need to reach out, that the best moments of your day can be standing on your porch, calling out to each other, singing to each other, the call and response of one another, the banging the drums made from family and friends with pots and pans to honour our first responders, and lifting up our voices together on porches or gathered around campfires. We have been telling stories since we began: it's what makes us human and allows us to know one another.

So I want to share the joy of storytelling with you now, but I also want to share some techniques with you so you, too, can feel more ready and prepared to keep this tradition alive. Get ready for a very sweet and meaningful collection of some of the most affirming, inspiring, and empowering stories I've ever had the pleasure of listening to. And then use my pro-tips on how you, too, can embrace the craft we're all born with but maybe need to tweak a little as we grow! Each of the storytellers who appears in these pages has agreed to share their stories with us, so gather around, Cousins. Let's spread joy!

Mahsi cho and with deep respect,
Richard Van Camp

LET'S GET COOKING AND SHARING

1.
A MIRACLE STORY

Let's start with something really powerful and let me also tell you something about myself that is important because it helps make me a good storyteller: *I believe in miracles.*

I really and truly do because I've been a part of so many, and I've had the joy of recording Elders and story-tellers who've lived them, witnessed them, recounted them.

I love asking people, "Have you ever been a part of a miracle?"

I'm never disappointed when strangers, audience members, neighbours, and friends who I thought I knew everything about start sharing that they, in fact, have.

Miracles, to me, affirm that there is a divinity at play around us, and miracles remind me to trust the Great Mystery.

Want to read one shared by Tomson Highway in 2004? First, let me introduce you to Tomson with his short biography—in his own words!

Tomson is the son of legendary caribou hunter and world championship dogsled racer, Joe Highway. He was born in a snow bank in north-ern Manitoba (god's truth!), where it meets Sas-katchewan and what is now called Nunavut, in December yet! Today, he makes his living writing plays, novels, and music. His best-known works, of many, are the plays, *The Rez Sisters*, *Dry Lips Oughta Move to Kapuskasing*, and *Rose*, as well as the novel *Kiss of the Fur Queen*, which spent some weeks on Canadian bestseller lists. He divides his year equally between a cottage on a lake in northern Ontario (Sudbury area) and an apart-ment in the south of France. Trained extremely well at an early age as a classical pianist, he still plays the instrument, most frequently in cabaret form (his own words and music), sometimes solo, sometimes with singer and musician friends in Europe, North America, and elsewhere.

Tomson's story is the perfect welcome to *Gather*. Enjoy 😊

***

THE TIME I FELL TO MY DEATH AND THREE GUARDIAN ANGELS FLEW DOWN FROM HEAVEN AND CAUGHT ME IN THEIR ARMS

You know, I was told by an Elder once that, from the Native point of view, there is no death, only "a going away." Death, in other words, is only a journey, a voy-age to another dimension of existence, another level of energy, if you will. When you die, that is to say, you go to another place, another position, on that great circle that is the life, and the rhythm, of the universe, a place from which you will rise again in another form at some other time, whether as a blade of grass, a leaf on a tree, a bird, or even something as simple as a ray of sunlight that falls on a naked human arm, a gust of wind, a rhythm, or a certain spark, an electrical bolt of pure energy. Which is why this Earth that we live on is, in and of itself, a miracle, a place of magic, a sacred space. Something like that. That's where I want to start my piece . . .

Last August of 2004, I was at a small party at the house of dear friends (of which I have about 3,000 on six continents, thanks to my three angels; it helps, of course, to be 53, not 23). The house that hosted this party was in Toronto, a house I had been to many times before, meaning to say that I knew, quite well, the struc-ture and design of this house (including its stairways!). I must say, however, that I had just come to this party from performing a show, a cabaret where I was the fea-tured pianist, and I therefore had shoes on that I never otherwise wore—my "show shoes" I call them—dress shoes, in other words, that have uncharacteristically slippery soles (I bought them in Turkey some two years ago). So *that* was one factor—that the soles of my shoes were extremely, unusually slippery. The second factor was that it was very late at night, perhaps two in the morning. And so we, of course, had been drinking. And smoking. Factor number three was that I had just given my all at this cabaret—my own music, my own lyrics, myself at the piano—for almost two hours non-stop, me acting as MC at the same time, so I was very tired. No. I stand corrected: I was exhausted because, in part, it had been the last show of several and this, in effect, was the wind-up celebration to a highly successful undertaking.

My friends and I, that is to say, were all in an excited, overly exhausted state. And factor number four was that we were on the deck at the back from which, in order to get to the washroom, one had to walk down these stairs that were not only extremely steep (you know, one of those stairways in these renovated old houses that are so steep they look like step-ladders), stairs that were not only extremely narrow, that were not only carpeted with a rather slippery carpet (especially for the kind of shoes I was wearing) . . . but these stairs, on top of all this, were unlit. They were almost completely in darkness.

So at one point in the early hours of the morning, on my way down that stairway, I slipped and I fell from the top to the bottom *of that stairway*. I took a spectacular plunging, five-metre dive, and fell right smack on my head. It was the same kind of fall that paralyzed Superman (the actor, Christopher Reeve, that is) for life and eventually killed him. It was the same kind of fall that another man my age had that same week, a famous British literary agent based in Edinburgh, Scotland and who died on the spot, at his own home no less. And me? You know what happened to me? I walked away from that fall. Not only that, but I played another show at another theatre (from the first one where we had played) just two nights later, wearing sun-glasses to hide one huge black eye, but, it made me feel like Ray Charles sitting up on that stage banging that keyboard.

All I remember from that fall is waking up in the CAT-scan machine at St. Michael's Hospital some six hours later. For the first half-second that I was awake, I thought I was in a coffin. And I remember this white light all around me. And then I remember having my face stitched by the most gentle of doctors. At that moment, no one knew—for the four friends from the party were there with me—no one knew if I would ever move a finger again in my life.

Me? Never in my life have I felt so at peace—with myself, with the world, and with life. I think that's what death must be like, you know, the most peaceful, beautiful feeling on Earth. I think, when you die, that you just kind of float away. And it's over. I don't think it's traumatic in the least, not for the person who's dying. Who it's traumatic for, quite on the other hand, is those people whom one leaves behind. But for you personally? I think you just float off into a most exquisite, unutterably beautiful . . . well . . . I don't think words exist for the concept in any human tongue. The experience, ultimately, is inexpressible.

Anyway, that fall happened back in August of 2004. It is now late February of 2005. So I've had time to think about it all. And I've thought about it a lot. And you know what I feel it was all about? I think that through some weird, unexplainable sort of *synergy*—some mystical exchange of energies, that is to say—that my three guardian angels flew down that stairway with me that night—my father, my mother, and my brother. And, let me tell you, these were fine, fine spirits—all three of them when they were alive, quite extraordinary, in fact. And I think that there, at the bottom of that stairway that night, they caught me. And laid me down to rest ever so gently. Because it was *not* time for me to go.

I didn't break an arm, a wrist, a hand, or a finger. I know: I'm a piano player. For piano players, and musicians in general, things like fingers and hands and wrists and arms are of the essence (which is why we make such bad fighters!). I didn't break my nose. I didn't even break, or even scratch my glasses. It seems they just sort of went flying and landed in a nice soft place.

I didn't crack my skull. Most important of all, however, I didn't break my neck, which I could very easily have done. All I ended up with was eight small stitches, three on the bridge of my nose. And five tiny ones in my right eyebrow so that the scar there is not even visible. And, two nights later, I walked on to the stage of that theatre. And played for almost a thousand people. My singer sang like an angel. I know, I saw and heard her from five feet away. My sax player played like one. And I? Well, I just played my best, even if I could see the keyboard of my grand piano with one eye only. And I thanked, as I played, over and over again, my three guardian angels, my wondrous trio of spirit guides, my late father, my late mother, and my late younger brother.

There's a lesson to be learned here, I think. And that is this: how very important it is to take care of those around you while they're still here with you. Because, after they're gone, after they've travelled on to that other place on that great circle, *they* will take care of *you*.

And *that's* my miracle.

Tomson Highway
Banyuls-sur-Mer, France
February 20, 2005

* * *

Mahsi cho, Tomson! Friends, remember this: We are not alone. Angels and spirit helpers are with us all. And this gathering together of stories, I hope, will help you when you need some medicine for renewal and inspiration and for peace.

2.
HEAVEN IS LIKE WEST EDMONTON MALL

I remember the day Dënesųłiné (Chipewyan) Elder Maria Brown told me she'd seen Heaven. I'd gone to pick her up for an appointment with the Handi-Bus that I was driving. You'll hear more about this bus later!

"Did I ever tell you about the time I died and saw Heaven, Richard?" she asked me. My jaw dropped. "No."

We had some time.

Maria told me a story that day that changed my life forever. Sadly I didn't have my tape recorder with me. But as I listened, I knew that I wanted the whole world to hear what she had witnessed and experienced.

"You want to know what Heaven is like, Richard?" She told me: "Heaven is like West Edmonton Mall. Everyone's young there."

I couldn't believe it.

She went on to tell me that she did see her parents and her husband, John Louie. Holy wow, I was floored.

She told me so much, and I just sat there taking it all in, so grateful. So, so grateful. I also wanted the world to know the message of the story: that we are all here for a purpose.

I went back a few days later and recorded her story. Thank goodness I did. I had it professionally transcribed, and I've done my best to keep the interviews in this book as true to the original conversation as possible with no words cut and as few explanations as possible, but sometimes imperfect recordings and the distance of time make meanings and words hard to distinguish. I take full responsibility for any errors that may have made their way into the transcriptions. If you would like to hear Maria in her own words, I uploaded her interview to my SoundCloud account (find the link in the Resources on page 189). Gosh, I miss her.

Here is the interview.

RICHARD: Maria, tell me when you were born.

MARIA: I was born 1923, September the 14th in Fitzgerald, Alberta.

R: And you're a Chipewyan Indian?

M: Yeah.

R: Do you speak your language?

M: Yeah.

R: Do you speak French?

M: No.

R: A little bit of Kitchen French?

M: No.

R: No?! Just Chip?

M: Yeah.

R: English?

M: Yeah.

R: Tell me about the time you saw Heaven.

M: Well, I don't know what happened that time. I had a lot of pain and I went to bed in Yellowknife three years ago. That'd be, what year is that? Nineteen . . .

R: Ninety-four.

M: Ninety-four, and I woke up and I went into this place, two girls standing there. Young, young girls. They have material. And it was silk, satin, velvet, lace. Beautiful colour, no black, no red. Just white, all different colour but all nice colour. And this girl says, "How much? That's nice, we don't have that. How much is material cost? We don't have any money and we don't buy nothin' here." And then I heard the voice saying, "She has to go, she can't stay."

And then this girl said, "Do you know Joe? You know Joe Mabillon, you guys call him Joe Mabillon. That's the one sitting there [with] Albert Jewell. Joe." And he was still big, but he was young. Albert Jewell was a young guy and teasing people with the same . . . like, something like the mall. And I looked down, was people walking around. They got beautiful clothes, beautiful. And I seen Joe Mabillon was there, royal blue suit on. And they had these handbags and was walking what I thought was a marble floor. And I turn around to these guys again and they said, "You have to go," she said. 'Cause I still hear this, and the speaker, it sounds like . . . And I said, "Why I have to go?" And she said, the first one standing, she said, "Because it's not your time." And I said, "Where I am?" I didn't say, "What do you mean, Roy?" or anything, I just said, "Where I am?"

And they says, "You're in Heaven."

"Oh, no," I says. "I don't want to go back. I want to see Jean-Louis, and I want to see my mom and dad." And they said there, "You can't because so many people, they still do like they doing here, but they're younger. You'll never recognize them." You know, that's the way this woman, this girl, said . . . It didn't say we're down, they says, "When we came I was seventy-four, she was seventy and she looked—it looked like they were only sixteen years old and they're so young."

R: Wow. And they were Native?

M: Yeah.

R: Native girls?

M: Yeah, Native girls. And then again I heard this: "She has to go." But I don't know how I got there. I didn't know that I went through that door, but . . . all at once I was right there where those two girls was standing. And there's people walking around and they were so pretty. They were so pretty and everybody— nobody ever seen an old person—all young. And then when I again heard this, "She has to go. She can't stay," and this girl said, "You got to go," then I turn around to the door. And there was a wide, wide door and there was a gold—just like there's still gold on it, and not even . . . there was silver. And I didn't touch the door and I woke up on my bed.

***

Maria and I talked of other things that day, and other days too she shared stories with me. But I never forgot that first story of Heaven. She ended it in this way:

M: We are all here for a purpose. We are all here be- cause it's our time here. When we're called, we're called Home.

R: Mahsi cho!

My goodness what a story. Thank you, Maria, for shar- ing it.

3.

WHAT IS IT ABOUT STORYTELLING THAT GETS THIS ANCIENT BLOOD OF MINE ROARING?

t's connection, community, and purpose, plain and simple. It's giving someone the same goose bumps I receive after I retell an incredible story that gives me a soul sigh. It's seeing someone tear up with a story I've retold that moves my heart, as well. It's being human; it's the gentle reminder that we are all children of the great mystery of life.

I am a storyteller, and I'm a good storyteller because I'm a good listener.

I am Tłı̨chǫ Dene. I was born and raised in Fort Smith, Northwest Territories in 1971, nickname and hickey capital of Canada where we can two-step to anything, anytime, anywhere. The Dënesųłıné (Chipewyan) name for Fort Smith is Thebacha, "beside the rapids." Fort Smith is a small community, primarily a Dene and Métis town, tucked into the boreal forest right next to the great Slave River and underneath a sky revered for the northern lights who return every winter and fall to mesmerize us with their nightly dance. The national park now even has one of the largest roaming buffalo herds!

I was raised in a time when families visited families. CBC Television was on for a few hours every day in black and white. A lot of it was in French. *The Edge of Night* was Canada's first soap, and I remember our babysitters—the Clarke sisters—screaming their heads off, waking my brother and me up in complete terror, every time the Bay City Rollers came on the television singing "Saturday Night." The members of KISS were gods; Tommy Hunter ruled. We knew how to host and be hosted. As kids we had something called G.O.D: The Great Outdoors. We were outside all the time. We were happy and we were healthy. Maybe it's the fact that we're all related through marriage, friendship—or maybe it's the eight-month winters—but holey canoley, Cousins, do we love to hear and share stories. I know we all do. Whether it's talking about sports, the weather, relationships, or local or international happenings, we all ache for stories because we ache for connection. We all crave community, and it is stories, once shared, that bond us.

Don't believe me about being the nickname capital of Canada? Check out some of the insightful names of our townies who have made Fort Smith such a lovely place to be from. I share these names with utmost respect: Duck Soup, Wolfman, Dudes, Georgie Porgie, Tsitsi, Bigman, Larry Boy, Pie Face, Wiener, Beefcake, Skrudi, Ogre, Bart, Jon Guy, Mav, Ice, Goose (yes, from Top Gun!), Garbage, Blue Eyes, Stinky, Gootch, Ivansky, Android, A-rod, Scooby, Freddy Boom Boom, Rubberman, Trapper, Smokie, Peanuts, Squeek, Pinto, Pistol, Eyebrows, Tuk Tuk, Earl the Pearl, Junior, Chang, Slim, Iron Mike, Tony Toenails, Pie Kennedy, Bobby One Leg, Boogie, Baby Boogie—I could go on and on, but Fort

Smith, I love you. I post these names of our townies past and present who have made our town magic with absolute admiration. I don't have a nickname—well, not that I know of!—so it's with a secret envy I sing your nicknames to the world.

No doubt you have heard how important the oral tradition and storytelling is to Indigenous communities. So let me tell you my origin story of how I became a storyteller and author: it can be traced to when I decided to volunteer to be the Handi-Bus driver for my hometown. On my first day of work, I knew with everything inside of me that I was the luckiest man in the world because I had the privilege of driving our Elders around town to where they needed and wanted to go. And with them came their stories. The smartest thing I ever did— besides marry Keavy Martin—was race to the Radio Shack in town to purchase a tape recorder and record our Elders with their permission. I'd record the stories, listen to them, transcribe them, and give them back to the Elders for their families. I'm still giving those stories out twenty-five years later to future generations of those Elders who are here now. And I've never stopped. From there, I went to the En'owkin Centre in Penticton, and I recorded our Elder-in-Residence Glen Douglas and our Office Manager Anna Tonasket. Everywhere I went, I would ask permission to record Elders, storytellers, and authors, and I must have at least forty stories recorded both on audio and videotape that I share all the time. Why? Well, because they're medicine!

And guess what? In this book, I'm going to give you the sweetest homework. I'm going to reaffirm what we already know and what COVID taught us or reminded us of: We need community, we deserve dear friends, and we don't need more stuff. Instead, we need more stories, more teachings, more visits, more feasts, more recipe sharing, more laughs, more cookouts, more shore lunches, more family songs, and more time with those who carry our hearts. And for all of it, the Great Outdoors is there for renewal and astonishment. "True food" is healing and mending, and it's what we crave and deserve.

Get ready to meet some of the finest storytellers that I've ever had the pleasure of recording and transcribing. And get ready to learn those tips and tricks of storytelling, visiting, and listening. I'm hoping that just by looking at this book on your shelf you'll honour the next full moon with a feast and a giveaway when stories will be swapped and sung and remembered so they can travel in the future. I'm hoping that if you're lonesome now, you won't be three full moons from now. I'm hoping that your family will honour one another with listening, asking, recording, and passing the stories forward. My wish for you is one of warmth: I wish for you everything you ache and wish for. I wish that the pandemic that we're all going through has taught us not only to reset and get back in touch with our priorities, but also that our survival depends on connection, and we connect best, most powerfully, through storytelling and sharing.

4.

WELCOME TO "THE GREYHOUND" AND WHY STORIES MATTER

I love my life. I love my family and our home. My wife, Keavy, our son, Edzazii, and I live in Edmonton, Alberta—Treaty 6 Territory—in the coolest neighbourhood of Old Strathcona. It's the coolest because everyone visits with just about everyone—even during COVID, we managed to visit responsibly with masks and social distancing in mind, and we did it because we knew we had to.

We know our neighbours; they know us—either through Play Group where I volunteered every Monday and Wednesday when I was a stay-at-home dad, the nursery school down the street that our son attended, soccer, birthday parties, cooking, feasting, or filling the bird houses every full moon together. Sometimes we met for gossip sessions at the counter at our local stores—Blush Lanes, Save-On-Foods, Bison Valley Variety Meats, the farmers' market, the Old Strathcona Edmonton Public Library, and Warp 1 for comics and graphic novels are a few of our weekly visiting stations—or at Tubby Park or at the water park or at King Edward Park, waving from our front porch, and I say hello to everybody. And of course, during COVID, we feel safe and taken care of in our community because we have already spent the time building community through visiting, spending time together, and swapping stories.

I am proud of our home and the garden my wife and son have created. My buddy Joel Duthie calls our house "The Greyhound" because, he said, whenever he drives by, there's always a pile of people sitting together eating, laughing, feasting. Now this was obviously before COVID had hit, but it's true: our house was like a bus stop with people coming and going! I take that as the ultimate compliment—in our home, pre-COVID (and, I know, post-COVID), there is always laughing, feasting, and soul nourishing stories.

Just tonight, I made the chili a little too spicy. I texted three neighbours asking if they wanted some, telling them I could leave it on their doorsteps: Chris and Kelly Fox texted back saying they had fresh mac and cheese coming out of the oven, so they were good. Dan was working and never got back to me. If I see him tomorrow, I have leftovers for him for his lunch. We share what we have. It's the least we can do to live the lives that we enjoy every single day.

The community we've built matters—this became even more apparent during the pandemic—and so we will never ever take each other for granted. We take care of each other. For instance our neighbours called us last week and asked if we could check on their stove. They were four hours away and had planned a weekend away. Eric was worried he'd left the stove on. I walked out, looked through their side balcony door. The stove was off. A quick text calmed their worries.

Our neighbour Don knocked on our door one night and woke us to let me know I'd left the garage door open. Whew. That would have been so sad to have discovered our bikes and food from the freezer gone. Our other neighbour Marvyn, a retired mechanic with the military, gave us a bike his granddaughter has grown out of and Edzazii loves it. He should be the right size for it next spring. With community, we build each other up. We feel safe.

Yesterday I made fresh bannock with cheese between the fried eggs and called our neighbours to come over and have a sample. Chris was on our doorsteps in seconds. I also always seem to need the one ingredient when cooking. I'm proud to be able to either call, text, or knock, and I can usually secure what's missing right away. I think I have three sets of keys from neighbours "just in case," and I'm pretty sure we've given our keys to three of ours, "just in case."

What does this have to do with storytelling, you might ask? Well, I'll say it again and again in this book: it's through stories that we've come to know each other. We trust each other because we've trusted each other with our stories. We know each other through our stories. Storytelling = connection = community = joy and comfort = health and survival.

5.
DISCONNECTION

One of the things I worry about is the fact that I keep seeing couples at restaurants where one or both parties are on their phones, quiet. How lame is that? And what a confusing time for our youth—I'm hearing more and more that kids in the city are more comfortable inside their houses than out. What they are doing inside? They, too, are looking at their screens. *The Globe and Mail* published an article saying that three out of five adults are lonely. Children must be too, I imagine.

It's never been easier to not leave the house after you work, and now you can get all your groceries and house needs delivered directly to your home. Mind you, this has been helpful during the pandemic, but without a doubt the virtual age is upon us. I'm proud that in our home, music is always on and we read books and chat at night before we snuggle up and dream together. Oh sure, we love *Downton Abbey*, *Nashville*, *Suits*,

Outlander, *Trickster*, and *Brooklyn Nine-Nine*. We love an episode a week—that's 48 minutes to make popcorn, sip kombucha or chaga (or both)—and it's so lovely to be swept away by epic storytelling with gorgeous visuals. It's also incredible to read and share stories with each other. Life is intoxicating when you have a great book, and it's incredible to follow fearless authors wherever they wish to take you. Some of my favourite books are *Son of a Trickster* by Eden Robinson and *Indiscretion* by Charles Dubow, but I read just about anything. I've been following *The Walking Dead*, the comic, by Robert Kirkman for over ten years now, and I'm always up for suggestions on what I should read next.

It's intoxicating when you share stories about these great books, the music you've been listening to, or the newest television series you've been watching. So here's an idea: if you feel like you're on the fade-out from friends, or if you are lonely for friends, family, stories, feasts, and gatherings, please start hosting in your home when it's safe, and until then on Zoom or some online gathering place. And enjoy "true food" together (healthy, locally grown, and prepared with TLC) or start buying gifts or making things for the friends and community you wish to honour. Who can say anything but "Yes!" to someone who calls and says, "Hey, uh, it's been too long since I saw you. I made something for you and your family. I was wondering if we could have a feast and I could stop by? It'd mean a lot to me to give this to you."

Or

"Hey, it's been way too long since we got together. I have a new recipe I've just tried. Can I bring it by and cook for you, and can we feast together on a date that works for you? I'll do all the cooking and I'll even wash up after." Our friend Jordan Carpenter did this for us years ago when we were new parents, and we've never forgotten it.

Or

"Hey, I heard that someone wants to fool around with you. Cook me supper, make me tea and I'll tell *all* as we dine and celebrate the Great Mystery together, Cousin!" (Ummm, yeah; that might only work in the North where I'm from, but you can try it.)

I'm convinced that we all need to share more stories and time together. We're not meant to raise our families alone. Nor are we meant to be connected more often to phones than to people. When we feast together, we celebrate the gift of life and become family through stories. Who doesn't want to know the stories of their grandparents and parents? Sitting down at the table and sharing meals and conversations is so essential for this bonding to occur and for the wisdom and folklore to pass from one generation to another. So cook for your parents, your cousins, your aunties, your children, your grandmother. And if you don't know how to cook? Well, I can help you out with that too!

6.
HOW TO BE A
GREAT COOK*

To become a great cook, all you need are the right ingredients the day before and time. It takes ten minutes to prepare a pork shoulder, onions, and the right mix of seasoning for an eleven-hour masterpiece in your crock pot for pulled pork on rice with a salad. It takes the same amount of time to prepare buffalo or baby back pork ribs. The key is preparation and time and lots of onions. It takes ten minutes to prepare lean ground beef, mixed with a great tomato sauce, three kinds of peppers, an onion, a clove of garlic, some spice, and carrots in a crock pot for four hours. Then stir it every hour to make the best sauce ever. Yesterday it took me sixty-five minutes and a few ingredients (chicken thighs, chicken stock, egg noodles, onions, carrots, celery, thyme, butter, and two bay leaves) to prepare homemade chicken noodle soup

----

*   *So You Can Set the Stage for Great Storytelling*

in the crock pot (I timed it—I'm a Virgo), and it was delicious and soul nourishing.

You can learn anything on YouTube these days—better to hear it from your uncles or aunties or parents—but YouTube can help too! So, gather around that fire, that cookstove, or that crock pot, and please enjoy cooking for your friends. If you want your house to become "The Greyhound" of your street like ours is, well, a crock pot, fresh ingredients, and time are all you need to start rocking out as much as you wish. And once you start cooking for others, sooner or later they'll have to start cooking for you. That is how humanity is supposed to work, isn't it?

7.
NOW YOU'RE COOKING

Okay, so you have the stew ready and you have guests to invite. Now you've got to get ready to tell some stories!

First lesson: To be a great storyteller, you've got to read the room or the dinner table and ask yourself before you even begin, "What kind of spirit am I going to leave everyone with if I share this?"

For example, if you start telling medical horror stories over supper with children present, well, chances are you're going to be labeled as "Captain Bringdown" and maybe will never be invited back. If you cross-friend and pit friends together who you know are anti this and anti that at your table, well, chances are your pro this and pro that friends are going to have a debate that'll go for hours and bore you to tears. Great food and knowing your audience—which folks are in the room—can help set the perfect setting for an evening of pure communion.

So, let's talk about knowing your audience. Do you know what "smearing" is? I learned this recently when I was on a tour. I learned from a police officer that smearing is when you share something with someone who does not have the resources to handle what you've shared. For example, if you are a doctor, chances are you are desensitized to a lot of thing the rest of us aren't. Most of us can't handle hearing about what you see in a single day. We can't. Think carefully and ask yourself, "Is there a chance I've smeared my family, friends and colleagues?" If so this could be a good time to apologize and make amends.

Oh! Make sure you do the dishes and tidy up while your friends are still there. There's nothing worse than having to clean up after friends leave and it's late and you're tired. If you're feasting at our house, you'll notice I've perfected the art of doing dishes as the night goes on. I'm happy to do it.

Maybe it's because when our parents were out of town when we were younger, my brother Roger threw "Ragers" and made everyone clean as they were partying in our log home. Can you imagine these big tough guys who came to party vacuuming and scrubbing our shower? Big tough guys would be like, "Geez, Roge. I came here with a two-six of Smirnoff to get snaked out of shape! I didn't come here to wash your shower and scrub toilets."

And my brother would be like, "Get to work. You got a time to lean, you got a time to clean." And they would!

That is pure brilliance right there, Cousins!

And put your cell phones away. Enjoy the evening. All of the messages and Facebook updates will be deliciously waiting for you when you get home.

Enjoy every visit because we never know what's coming. As I get on in years, I find joy in savouring moments, friendship, family, travel, and feasts.

Mahsi cho.

8.

LISTEN AND VOLUNTEER

Now who am I?

As far as I know, I'm the first published member of the Tłıchǫ Dene to ever publish a novel, a comic book, a graphic novel, and a collection of short stories. I believe there were a few Tłıchǫ authors who've written children's books, but as far as I know I'm one of the humble trailbreakers in the Northwest Territories who've done their part of welcoming the world into our homes, lives, and cultures—all through our literature. One of my novels, *The Lesser Blessed*, is now a feature film with First Generation Films. You can watch it on HBO, Netflix, Amazon Prime, Shaw On Demand, iTunes, APTN, and CBC. I currently have four short movies based on my short stories out: *Mohawk Midnight Runners*, based on my short story "Dogrib Midnight Runners" in *The Moon of Letting Go*; *firebear called them faith healers*; *Hickey Gone Wrong*, based on my comic with Christopher Auchter; and *Three Feathers*, based on a graphic novel that I wrote with Krystal Mateus as the artist. We've also made *Three Feathers* into a full-length movie; it's the only movie that's been shot and released in four languages: Bush Cree, Dene, South Slavey, and English. There's actually a fifth language in there, but you have to see the movie to believe it. 🙂

One of my graphic novels with Scott Henderson, *A Blanket of Butterflies*, was a finalist for an Eisner Award in 2016. We lost out to *Silver Surfer*. What an honour: THE SILVER SURFER!!

How have I been able to do this? I listened. That's right. Because of my role as a listener, I've been able to publish twenty-five books in twenty-four years. One of my baby books, *Welcome Song for Baby*, was given out to every newborn baby in British Columbia in 2012 as part of the Books for BC Babies Program. That's 65,000 copies! But more so, I have listened to the Elders and the storytellers of my home community. I'm entirely convinced that had it not been for my Elders and my hometown of Fort Smith, I would not be the writer, storyteller, husband, father, neighbour, friend, son, and gossip that I enjoy being today.

And, as I said earlier (a good storyteller repeats the important parts!), the smartest thing I ever did—besides marrying Keavy—was to volunteer when I was nineteen years old in Fort Smith to drive the Handi-Bus. I was going to drive Fort Smith's Elders around to physiotherapy, Kaeser's every Thursday and the Northern Store every Friday, and to bingo, bingo, and more bingo. Here is where I learned what it meant to be a northerner, a Fort Smither, and a young Tłı̨chǫ man.

It was our Elders like Irene Sanderson, Maria Brown, Emilia Gratrix, Rosa Mercredi, Dora Tourangeau, Seraphine Evans, and Helena Mandeville who truly took me under their wings. Through countless hours of listening and laughing, and sharing, it was our town matriarchs who I learned to listen from. It's where I became a Listener.

As I listened to them share Spirit stories, ghost stories, creation stories, heartache and heartbreak stories, relationship/community (gossip) stories, and teaching stories—that's when I realized just how rich our town and people were. I remember racing to Radio Shack in Fort Smith and buying a tiny tape recorder. From there I would go back to the Elders and start recording them one by one. Thank goodness I did because I managed to tape my heroes and, thankfully, after transcribing their stories word for word, I was able to share them with their families and relations. This passion for recording Elders spread, and I now over have twenty-four stories that I've collected over the past twenty-four years; they are all treasures. I've shared my favourite stories that I felt were the perfect match for *Gather*, and I hope they astound and inspire you.

But it wasn't only Elders' stories that I was sharing with family and friends. I realized that, deep down, what the Elders were sharing with me were things they were worried we, as future generations, would forget. Our storytelling tradition has always been strong, and stories pass our knowledge and values and our hope for a better world from generation to generation.

You can read their influence in all my books. I could not have written any of my short stories, novels, or children's books without my Elders' knowledge, insight, and grace. I'm indebted to my Elders like Tomson Highway, Jace DeCory, Fred Beaulieu and Maggie Sikyea, Barb and Richard Mercredi, Earl and Marlene Evans, Mike Beaver, Henry and Eileen Beaver, Glen Douglas, and my fellow storytellers who have made me howl with laughter, blush with "Ummmmmm," and soar with inspiration. In the back of all my books, I have a closing chapter titled "Afterwords" in which I acknowledge where each of the stories came from. If you are a fan of my work, check it out. If you don't know anything about my writing, now you know I'm inspired by stories every single day—either in my retelling or in my writing.

Stories are my fuel. Stories are my medicine. Stories are my way of honouring my Elders and the stories that they've shared with me because those Elders and those stories have helped guide my life. But please remember, you have to know *how* to listen. And that it is *active* not passive listening. Look at the eyes, faces, and hands of the storytellers as they speak and tell their stories (well, unless you are driving the Handi-Bus!). And always put down your phone when they are talking to you so you truly can listen, see, and *hear* them. That is how you *honour* them.

9.
EMBRACE THE TECHNOLOGY / SHARE THE STORIES

Okay. Put down your phone. Put down your phone. Ummmmmmm. But wait. It's true, technology is not all bad. We certainly learned how much we need it with COVID. It does have forces for good. And what's cool in my life now is I have a boombox that can convert the recordings I made on cassette tapes back in 1991 and turn them into MP3s. I've been able to email recordings to descendants and loved ones starting back in 1991 and 1992 when I was the Handi-Bus driver for Fort Smith. Imagine hearing the laughter and stories of your Ancestors and being able to pass these along forever. What a divine gift.

I've been able to share the stories of Seraphine Evans talking about how the design of the Roman Catholic church in Fort Smith (where my brothers and I used to be altar boys) came to Bishop Trocellier in a dream.

I've been able to share the story of Trevor Evans (her grandson) sharing the story of the haunted woodstove that terrorized his family in the early '70s.

I've been able to share stories here and elsewhere of Rosa Mercredi talking about respect for animals, especially dogs.

I've been able to share a radio show I used to have with my good buddy Dylan Vasas in Yellowknife in 1991. We were called "Malcolm and Henry's Hour of Power" and we had eight shows, I believe. Thank goodness I kept the recordings of our show. We were college radio before we even knew what that was. We played The Sisters of Mercy, Siouxsie and the Banshees, RevCo, Ministry, Sons of Freedom, Nick Cave and the Bad Seeds, The Smiths. Man, we were the best!

I've been able to share the love story of how my grandfather, Joe Van Camp, on his first night on shore in Hollywood, California (October 6, 1945) right after the war, met his future wife, Helen Madden. Six weeks later, they got married. My grandmother was from Flint, Michigan. Grandpa Van Camp was the Chief Financial Officer at Stokely Van Camp. He served as a navigator in the Navy on the USS *Crouter*. I am grateful to my aunty Ann Van Camp for sending me this additional information. I had no idea my grandmother was from Flint. I knew my grandfather served in the Navy, but I did not know he was a navigator. These stories form who I am and connect me to people and places. What about you?

The stories you're about to read—some spiritual, some funny, some healing—were recorded with a simple request from me: "Can you tell me a story that will bring others hope or joy? Make someone laugh or be more cautious? Can you tell me a story where you feel you have been part of a miracle?"

It has been a joy to email the audio recordings back to the storytellers years or decades later in a format they can upload and email and share with their grand-children and families. It's also been a joy to share with permission the stories of Glen Douglas, Maria Brown, and Anna Tonasket online for you to listen to in their own words on my SoundCloud account. Check them out. You can hear the emotion in their stories. Listen to those pauses. See how they use calm and timing to deliver the stories that helped forge my life. You can do this, too. The message of this book is simple: Do not wait to record your Elders, Knowledge Keepers, and heroes. Their families and future generations will thank you.

When your life becomes about giving instead of taking, your life becomes rich and the world becomes a far brighter place. Stories can help make it so.

That's how I want to be remembered: as someone who shared all that he could in a good way, including many, many, many good stories!

Mahsi cho!

10.

CAMPING CHALLENGE

I want to share a story that happened on September 8, 2017, on my forty-sixth birthday.

That day (or once upon a time), I was in the presence of a master as our plumbing was being inspected. The plumber (I should have asked his name) was talking about having deer in his front and back yards outside of Red Deer, Alberta. He was also telling me that he was gearing up for another camping trip with his friends. There'd be kids, family, stories, campfires, great food, and stars for miles. He also told me they all bring generators for the kids.

"Oh," I said. "So everyone can charge their phones and iPads?"

"No," he said firmly. "We have a rule. All phones stay in the cars. We use generators to charge the electric trucks and cars for the kids. This is our time to reconnect as couples and friends."

Brilliant!

How many of us could accept the challenge of not having our phones handy if we all went camping together? How many of us could go camping where we all prepare meals together; keep the sacred fire burning; share stories, songs, and traditions; learn to try new skills; be there for each other; build memories; share laughs; lighten sorrows; connect; reconnect; and just be?

The summer of 2018 was the year my family started camping. Now that our son is out of the Ewok stage, it's so much easier to enjoy camping because Edzazii wants to help. Usually we arrive and I get to work cooking as my wife and son set up our tent. When it's up, we feast. I wash up as they take off to the playground or beach and then I secure the wood. I cut kindling and stack the wood high, and then I start cooking on our grill. The best part of camping is having fun—the food, reconnecting with each other and meeting our camp neighbours, sharing the day together, and noticing what's happening seasonally are important. I have taken the best photos of our family while camping at Lesser Slave Lake in Jasper. You could spend every weekend camping in Alberta and British Columbia or anywhere and never get tired of the beauty around you. This is in your DNA—to be outside, to feast and gather around the fire and build the memories that will be so cherished forever in the stories and songs that will be passed on in your family's future.

11.
BEING A GUEST: WHAT TO BRING

Cousins, I hope you are enjoying what you're reading so far and that I'm not being cheap to you. Here is what I recommend you bring when you go be a guest and a listener of storytellers:

1. Tobacco to show respect. You can bring it in a pouch or in a pack of cigarettes. We do this to be respectful. Tobacco is used in ceremony and it's not my place here to talk about why, but this is a gift to show respect in Indigenous communities. I'll have my Elder Eileen Beaver tell you more about this later in the book. For now, know to bring it for respect.

2. Food. Why not bring an Elder their favourite fish or country foods? Do it! My friend Katrina Chappell reminded me that "it's more than just the food itself. It's the contact. It's the connection." It's the special feeling of knowing that

someone really and truly is taking and making the time for you. Plus, it just feels great to do this.

3. Medicines or teas you've grown and/or picked or have gathered in a good way for sharing.

4. Candles.

5. Berries.

6. Dessert.

7. Flour.

8. Coffee.

9. Lard.

10. Sugar.

11. Money.

12. Hope. Always be careful of the news, stories, and spirit that you bring into an Elder's home.

13. Regift a gift you were given but never used. It might be fun to just say, "I was given this blender a long time ago and, you know, we never even opened it. I thought you could use it. If not, feel free to regift it. Pass it along."

14. A new mug.

15. Your new favourite CD.

16. Your new favourite book.

17. Your favourite tea.

18. Your favourite hot chocolate.

19. Your favourite coffee.

20. Your homegrown magic from your garden. Just last night, our neighbour Steve asked if we needed anything from his garden (potatoes, carrots, etc.), and I couldn't help but soul beam.

21. Your help. If you show up and someone needs help chopping wood or weeding a garden, please help them. They'll be grateful and will enjoy the company and you'll both share a moment.

22. Your attention. Remember to listen, not just with your ears but with your entire body. Watch how a storyteller paces themselves and lives in the silence between the big moments. Watch their hands, their tone shifts, how they change their voices to become the story.

23. Your stories, songs, and prayers. Make sure they are something you care about and would like to share.

12.
BEING A GOOD GUEST: WHAT TO DO

I sn't it the absolute best when someone is going to host you? It's even better when they tell you to not bring anything: "Just show up with an appetite." Holy canoley, it is the best. So, what do you bring for a visit and a feast? Here are a few suggestions.

1. Protocol: Alcohol has ruined so many lives. Please ask if you can bring wine or other alcoholic gifts before you do. It might be best to bring sparkly non-alcoholic beverages for your hosts just to be respectful.
2. **Cultural Protocol to the max.** Never interrupt a storyteller when they get going. If you continually interrupt someone when they're sharing their best, chances are you won't be invited back into their home or circle and/or, chances are you won't be welcomed back into what could have been yours. Mahsi.

3. Take off your hat when you're in someone's house. Trust me on this.

4. Keep your phone off. Don't take it out and don't ask for the password to someone's wireless signal seconds after sitting down. You're there to visit, not zombie out.

5. Please observe the local protocol when you travel. For example, one of the greatest insults you can do when you're in Bali is show the bottom of your feet to someone.

6. Be careful asking if someone "has any good news in the baby department." Many couples have fertility challenges and, sadly, many experience miscarriages. This could be a quick end to what could have been a great evening.

7. If anyone in your family is sick, cancel. Trust me: every parent can do the mental math of who showed up to their house a few nights ago when their child wakes up with a cold. (Even if the math doesn't add up biologically, we all do our own math when we're looking for someone to blame.) I remember one time our son had a bad cough, so we had to cancel a playdate. I was honest and the text I received was immediate: "Thanks for not sharing the cold!"

8. Don't waste food. If your kids aren't big eaters, offer to take their leftovers home.

9. Do the dishes.

10. Do not stay too late.

13.
WHERE IS YOUR TELEVISION?

Our Ancestors are known to be great story-tellers. But think about this also: we had very little TV! No social media! No phones! Our stories could carry on for days, especially in the winter during the long, dark nights. But we knew how to make the best of it and to survive. We visited. We did not Netflix and chill! 😊

When Keavy and I moved into our home in Edmonton, I was and wasn't surprised that the builder had installed television sockets across from where the bed would be and in both the upstairs and downstairs main living spaces.

Had we installed three televisions in these locations we'd be miserable. Why? I bet you that we wouldn't talk, listen to music, laugh, dance, play, and connect as much as we do right now. Our "television" sets are the three big windows we look out of all day every day together as our neighbours walk by and wave.

I was just remarking yesterday that if we look south in March in Edmonton, the moon is outside our door every morning. At night Venus is in the exact same spot.

How you say "Venus" in Bush Cree is ogeenanz. The late Dora Grandjambe in Fort MacKay taught me that.

How you say "Moon" in Chipewyan is kalazaa. Archie Smith in Fort Smith taught me that.

I never forgot when Fort Smith Elder Earl Evans called televisions "culture killers." I also think they are major disruptors to family. This summer I noticed that our son was playing in the yard at 9:10 in the morning and he was still outside at 7:10 at night after going to Tubby Park and the splash park and visiting with neighbours and friends. Now that is a full day.

If we had TV on all the time, well, I don't think we would be as happy as we are.

A friend recently told me that if you have the news on all the time in your home it's like drinking poison. Harsh, but that feels true! Ask yourself what kind of stories are around you. Of course we need to be informed, but we also have to limit information overload!

Indeed, if TV is separating the natural flow of your family, maybe it's time to do what we did with our TV sockets—cover them with artwork on the main floor and in our bedroom. We do have a TV in the basement, but that's for company when they "camp over" or stay with us downstairs.

There is a saying that those families who bought televisions in the '70s, well, those were the families who stopped visiting first.

When you don't have a TV, you go out of your way to visit, to gather stories, and to share them.

I like that.

Connection fills my love cup.

Where is your TV located?

And is your cell phone disrupting your life? There was a joke that went viral online. It basically said the most popular sexual position for couples is "The 11": it's when lovers lie side by side checking their emails, Facebook, Twitter, Instagram, etc. for hours and hours before falling asleep.

If you're one of those dads who wears an earpiece in your ear socket as you eat supper with your family at a restaurant while your kids are on their phones and your wife is staring off in the distance thinking of what could have been, well, this is your chance to reconnect with family, friends, community, hobbies, and life. Unplug, buddy.

Why not start sharing your stories with your kids? Why not share what you remember about the birth of your children and the miracle of your wife? Do your kids know their birth story? Do you know your own birth story? Why not let everyone in on how scared you were; how you broke down crying you were so worried; how, hours later when Baby finally arrived, you sang and wept and gave thanks for the sweet miracle of a new soul who chose you?

Do your children know how you two love birds met? What's your love story? Share it and share it often. Humble yourself with the stories of love you share with your family. Don't cheap out.

14.
GET CONNECTING

Storytellers need to share, and listening to Knowledge Keepers is how we inhale the universe. So get to it. Here are twenty-eight things you can do right now to get out, find new friends and stories, and help build community. This is also a gentle reminder to rekindle old friendships. And a not-so-gentle reminder that if COVID is still with us to WEAR A MASK, SOCIAL DISTANCE, AND BE SAFE!

1. Volunteer at a shelter, nursing home, or church, or be like me and volunteer to be a Handi-Bus driver.
2. Go to a mixer. Look in the back of your local newspaper and, chances are, there are mixers.
3. Join Toastmasters. Why not get on up and learn from your local group how to deliver a speech with authority and clarity?

4. Attend a support group to listen, share, and learn.
5. Go speed dating. Why not?
6. Ask your local library or the farmers' market or community garden if they need help.
7. Go to open microphone sessions for storytelling, poetry slams, literary readings, and panel discussions. Go as a watcher and listener. See how each presenter rocks out. Pick up their tricks and learn what's not working.
8. Go to live music. Chances are the folks who are around you are into what you're into. The icebreaker is the event. Perhaps you know something about the band that others don't? Why not casually drop that into the conversation?
9. Get started in philanthropy. Is there a cause you believe in? Why not start a group that focuses on helping financially or by serving?
10. Start a group that needs to address something that you are passionate about. I'll give you an example. Twelve years ago in Yellowknife, there were a few of us who were grumbling about having to travel down south to see our favourite writers perform. At the same time writers like George Blondin, Robert Arthur Alexie, Fran Hurcomb, Annelies Pool, Patti-Kay Hamilton, Jamie Bastedo, and myself were blazing our own trails as authors from the North. So, we decided to start our own group: NorthWords. For the past fifteen years we've brought some of Canada's most elite writers and storytellers to the North, and we're growing. We saw a need and we delivered. Each year we seem to

just get better and better; we could not have done it without our board members, volunteers, sponsors, and audiences. Mahsi cho to everyone who's come out to celebrate great stories with us. Have we all made new friends and contacts by serving and volunteering? You bet we have!

11. Go to church or start attending ceremony that speaks to your spirit.

12. Volunteer at an airport. I love airports—especially the Arrivals area. You see tearful reunions, smooch fests, make-out sessions, grandkids running for their grandparents, everyone done up for each other. I've even seen signs that potential grooms are getting ready to propose.

13. Contact friends you adore and prepare a meal and a reunion when there is an event coming to your community that you are all interested in. I'll give you an example. I once contacted four friends who love comics, action figures, and pop culture just as much as I do and asked them to join me for the Edmonton Expo so we could gallivant around and explore this annual celebration of all things Nerd Culture. I did it by email, and it was so much fun. Organizers for events such as the Edmonton Expo are always looking for volunteers. Folk on the Rocks, Yellowknife's very own music festival, is already looking for volunteers for next year.

14. Join a social, political, or pop culture movement—remember Pokémon GO? That took the world by storm. But hey, anything that gets people outside laughing and building community seems like a very human thing to do when we have an epidemic of loneliness that is made

worse with the COVID pandemic that heightens the loneliness. Even if you don't want to play these types of games, I'm always happy to ask, "What level are you at?" I had a young man tell me during the Pokémon GO era: "For people like me who have social anxiety disorder, it's the perfect way for me to get outside and meet people." Brilliant! I can't wait to hear about what the new thing will be!

15. Make friends at the park when you see another dad or mom with their kids and you have your own on full display. I usually go up and extend my hand and say, "Hi, Mom. How are you?" Or "Hey, Dad. How's things?" If I sense there's a chance to chat, I'll say, "How old is your little one?" From there I'll ask, "So are you excited about the new (fill in the blank of an upcoming movie that seems appropriate to ask about)?" From there, I'll get right to it: "So have you ever had to fight another man or woman for your man, or what?" I know—pretty forward. It's a reminder that there's really no time for small talk. Sometimes the response will be, "Whoa. Have I got a story for you"—and there we are. I'm lucky: I write books for all ages so I have an "in." Chances are that once someone knows you're a children's author, well, you can't be all that bad—I hope! Yes, no small talk. You can start slow but build quick. This way you know if someone's eager for some great stories, great laughs, and cool times. Once you share a great story with someone that leaves them laughing, chances are they'll want to visit with you the next time they see you.

16. Get out of the house, out of your comfort zone, and into situations where you're meeting like-minded people. Why not sign up for a first aid course? Why not sign up for a bush survival course? Why not take an evening class or a weekend class? It's all out there if you want it. And you know what I'll say here—if there is COVID, be smart about it!

17. Start a reading group. Host a book or movie club. Get everyone to host a different book in their home each month. Bring food and snacks. Make it a potluck. Chances are it's never really about the book or movie—it's about the community and friendship.

18. Start a storytelling group. Again, try and make this around a firepit, if possible. Get outside and sit in a circle. See what happens. It might be great to have a theme for each gathering: "Spirit Stories Night," "Miracle Stories Night," etc.

19. Start a stargazing group and get on out there and camp out together.

20. Bonus: get a dog. With all the walking and visiting you'll do three or four times a day, you'll have your own route and community.

21. Start a writing, knitting, quilting, moccasin making, costume making, etc., etc. group. Decide to meet every full moon in your home or take turns hosting.

22. Cook for your Elder(s) and bring them food and sit and visit with them once a week or offer to take them shopping, to an appointment, or to a social outing.

23. Volunteer to be a snow angel and a leaf angel where you show up and take care of an Elder's

yard in exchange for, well, just being helpful and being in service and of service.

24. Go to the movies again. Not only is this a great way to meet up with friends who you haven't seen in a while, I end up speaking to everyone in the lineup at the concession—I speak to the three people who I buy my ticket from, who check me in, and who prepare my snack. Then there's always the carpooling after. I find that's when we get a lot of visiting done.

25. Organize a singalong, a karaoke night, a talent show—even if it's on Zoom.

26. Especially during COVID, send letters and care packages. I hit the post office three times a week and enjoy sharing stories (if there's time) with the clerks. I also love receiving letters. Bring on the pen pals!

27. Remember whose birthday you missed. Cook for them and surprise them, even if it's weeks or months later. Trust me, they won't be sad.

28. Pick up the phone. Log onto FaceTime. Open Zoom, Facebook Messenger, or Skype. Call friends from your past. Call friends you're worried about. Call friends you miss and tell them so.

15.
BE REAL

Storytelling is giving and taking. And it should be more giving than taking. Remember that the guests who pitch in while attending our feasts are the ones we invite back!

What I mean is that you, as a storyteller and as a guest of a storyteller, need to be aware of what energy, laughter, stories, spirit, happiness, hope, food, helping hands, and shared memories you bring to the circle, campfire, or table.

Someone once told me that blood is thicker than water when it comes to family, but I don't think it's true. I think time is thicker than blood.

It's the time we share with each other that is the treasure.

Look back at all the friends who've given you the fade out. Is it because you weren't pitching in? Did you not bring stories, food, laughter, gifts, helping hands, energy, light, etc.? What are you bringing to the party?

If you're wincing as you read this, why not have a redo? Make a dish and host or bring gifts and food and host at your friend's home. And always be mindful of what stories you're sharing and what spirit you're bringing.

Being real, to me, is something I do when I visit. If someone offers vulnerability, I welcome their courage. If someone's struggling with something and lets me in about it, I listen and share my struggles, too. If someone needs a good laugh, I do my best. If someone just wants to hang out, we can do that, too. The key is to be there, be present, be real, be you. Meet friends halfway with where they're at. Sit with someone. Bring your best for them and they'll never forget it. What you give is what you'll receive. Even if it's not from them, it will be from the sweetest heart of you.

16.
BE CURIOUS

'm giving you homework right now: I want you to start asking people about your local calendar. What's happening in town and out of town? My reason is there's nothing like talking about wildlife to unite you as neighbours. There's also nothing like having to go to wildlife officers, national park officers, gardeners, hunters, birders, farmers, Elders, and Knowledge Keepers and ask, "So, um, what's happening this month in the bush and in our community?"

Growing up in Fort Smith, we had and still have pelicans, sandhill cranes, whooping cranes, black bears, brown bears, cinnamon bears, buffalo out west, and bison out east in Wood Buffalo Park. David King, Chipewyan and champion bush cook, once shared with our family that a bear always knows what you're thinking.

I'm sure you've all heard that if you put your shoes on the wrong feet and wear your turned jacket inside out and backwards that a bear will follow you home.

I live and breathe for this kind of knowledge and wonder. My grandfather Pierre Wah-shee was hesitant to even speak about wolverines because he had so much respect for them, but he did say, "Those who the wolverine touch . . . don't live long." Pierre did not speak English, and this was told to me through a translator— my mom. And I'm sure you've all heard the old ones say that a wolverine can steal your shadow. We need to hear more stories about the four-legged, the winged ones, those who crawl on the earth, and those who swim because it's through these teachings and stories that we learn how to respect them and so how to help them. And we use animal stories to warn our children. These stories essentially keep both the wolverine and the young children safe when out on the land.

17.
A GOOD STORYTELLER
IS MINDFUL OF TIME

S o that's your first piece of homework: start a calendar and start asking your neighbours, friends and family, and community and local park organizations what the shindig is with local animals. Do it. It's fun. Get your family to add to it. This way you have a bank of local knowledge you can share at the drop of a hat.

I'll give you an example. While in Honolulu for the Native American and Indigenous Scholars Association 2016 conference, our son turned two under the full moon. I learned through visiting with local folks who lived in Kona that it's usually ten to twelve days after the full moon that the jellyfish (or "jellies") return. Isn't that something? They follow the first quarter of the moon. Now that I've heard this, I can share it wherever I travel. I love this kind of info because it's great gossip and it can be used to "fish" for more info on other animals. Plus it helps keep us safe in the water, knowing when to go in and when not to go in!

There is nothing like surprising someone with pearls of information about animals and seasonal migration patterns. Do it! Having not only the local knowledge of the people but also of the animals and plants is key for telling good stories. Travellers love it if you can answer all their questions of *what is this?* and *what is that?* But be sure it's appropriate to tell them; know which stories are yours to tell and which are not to be shared with others. In fact, if you get started with a community calendar, you are not only a good storyteller in the making, but you're also becoming a land, water, and life protector. And the world needs more of you and me to witness and document the changes!

I'll get you started with my own calendar that I've been working on for years; I add to it all the time. Mahsi cho to everyone who's helped me. You know who you are, and I've listed the names of my Elders beside each pearl of knowledge. And if you want to send me more information, please do!

***

CALENDAR FOR MY HOMETOWN OF FORT SMITH, NWT

"So many caribou, they were like carpet on the lake."
–Archie Smith, on Tulsan Bay in the early '50s

May and June
ICE BREAKING UP TIME

- In the middle of May, there is a Salt River run of suckers. "Dry fish was made at this time." —Richard and Barb Mercredi

- Hunting for muskrats and beaver during the spring hunt. —Mike Beaver
- You can pick plants like spruce gum and rat root for medicine.
- Birch bark for baskets and canoes can be collected.
- You can go bird hunting for grouse, ptarmigan, duck, goose, and cranes during the spring hunt. —Richard and Barb Mercredi. Some of us do it all year round!
- Watch the NHL Playoffs!
- The little orange buffalo calves are born in April or May. —Mike Beaver
- Wolves are raising their pups in their dens.
- Caribou cows lose their antlers after the calves are born.
- Ducks and geese and prairie chickens lay eggs in May. —Archie Smith
- "People don't hunt beaver after Treaty time" (the day that Treaty payments that honour the Treaty 8 and Treaty 11 payments of 1899 and 1921 respectively are distributed). —Archie Smith
- "March to May is the best time to trap beaver, muskrats" for food and fur. —Archie Smith
- "People return from the land before Treaty (time)." —Archie Smith
- Pickerel fishing from May 15 to 30. —Richard and Barb Mercredi
- Cut firewood. —Richard and Barb Mercredi
- Make fishnet from gill net twine. —Richard and Barb Mercredi
- "Tapping birch trees for birch water sap." —Dot Desjarlais

- "April to June hunting, May 10 abouts."
  —Maggie Sikyea and Fred Beaulieu
- "Cut and peel logs in June. The trees would be thawed out so it would be easy to peel."
  —Mike Beaver
- "The trappers that use ratroot would bring it home. Wild peppermint tea." —Mike Beaver
- "The first bird that comes in the spring is the bald eagle. The first part of April. Sandhill cranes return the first of May and seagulls, too." —Fred Beaulieu

June to August
WHEN THE WATER AND SUN ARE WARM

- Waterways open during June.
- Beaver hunters return to their families after Treat Day. Everybody has a good time.
- **National Aboriginal Day on June 21, eh. Take a break and give 'er!**
- Tan hides.
- Make hide teepees.
- Forest fire season.
- Strawberries are good in July. "Got to pick them when they're ripe because they dry up."
  —Mike Beaver
- You can try mooching fresh strawberry jam from your granny's house!
- Some people hunt in the summer. People still hunt buffalo because they get the two- to three-year-old bulls. —Mike Beaver
- The men set nets for pickerel, whitefish, connie, or Jacks. —Mike Beaver

- Hunt moose in rivers because that's when there's a lot of flies and the moose go in the water to avoid them. —Mike Beaver
- From late June to early August, women dry fish while the men go hunting.
- Gather plants, roots, berries, spruce gum, and tamarack bark.
- Canoe building.
- Drying meat.
- High bush cranberries and saskatoon berries are ready at the end of July. Don't wait too long or they will dry up.
- This is the best weather for fishing in the Slave River. But the best time for fishing in the lakes is when the ice goes out in the spring and before freeze-up in the fall. That's when the lakes turn over (that means they circulate from top to bottom) and the big trout come up into shallower water from down in the deeps.
- When the wolf pups get too frisky for their dens, they get moved to rendezvous sites and then start moving around with the adults.
- "By the middle of the summer, the buffalo calves start turning from orange to brown. By the end of August, only the late calves are still orange." —Mike Beaver
- By the middle of August, the buffalo rut is on. They move around and get into larger groups. They are most likely to hang around near the highways and get into trouble with the traffic.
- "Strawberries in July." —Maggie Sikyea and Fred Beaulieu

- "Did you know that when a buffalo is killed in the summer, the rest of them would gather around it and push or smell it for quite a while? We have to chase them away to skin the downed buffalo. Must be their way of saying goodbye." —Mike Beaver

August and September
WHEN IT GETS DARKER

- Pick your berries. Cranberries are great in September.
- Make dry meat for sure as there's no flies. —Richard Mercredi
- Northern lights come back to us for the winter.
- Geese or duck hunting in September. —Mike Beaver
- People hunt bears to make grease before they go in the hole in late October and when they're just fat! —Mike Beaver
- Wolf pups that are too small get left behind by their packs. The big strong pups run with the adults and start learning how to hunt. "They learn to hunt when they're big enough [from] their mothers." —Mike Beaver
- Buffalo calves have to be able to keep up with their mothers. The cow and calf groups break into smaller herds and start moving to winter ranges. Red calves are rare; most have turned dark brown like the adults. "The mothers look after the calves 'til they can fend for themselves." —Mike Beaver
- Caribou and moose antlers are in velvet.

- "Blueberries, end of September. Cranberries, too. Gooseberries in August, right after strawberries in July. Saskatoons in August." —Maggie Sikyea and Fred Beaulieu
- "Sandhill cranes go back south in the early part of August as soon as the little ones start flying." —Fred Beaulieu

September and October
WHEN THE WIND GETS COLD /
WHEN THE MOOSE MEETS ITS MATE

- "That's when the velvet falls off [moose antlers] and the rutting starts." —Mike Beaver
- Richard Van Camp's birthday on September 8. Virgo, hey.
- The NHL starts around the first of October!
- Make snowshoes, toboggans, toboggan bags, and dog harnesses.
- Duck and geese hunting in September before they fly south.
- Blueberries are good from September to freeze-up when they get frost. Then they fall off.
- The small, weak wolf pups die.
- Buffalo hides get thick and then they grow their full winter coat.
- Caribou start moving back into the trees.

October to February
FREEZE-UP

- Get your wood for the long winter.

- Trapping time (squirrel, weasel, mink, fox, wolf, lynx, wolverine, beaver, marten, otter).
- The wolves are busy trying to catch buffalo calves or corner older buffalo that get left behind by their herds. Sometimes the wolves even go after prime bulls. It might take days or weeks to wound and finally kill their prey.
- The buffalo are busy pushing snow out of the way with their huge faces so they can feed on the green sedges that are frozen under the snow in the wet meadows. When the wolves get too bothersome, the buffalo might move long distances to get away.
- Caribou rut in late November, and the bulls lose their antlers around Christmas time.
- "Put up hung fish for dogs' feed as well as eating. Dry meat made in winter for summer as well as marrow grease, dry lace fat, and fat (smoked)." —Richard and Barb Mercredi

November to February
WHEN THE DAYS ARE SHORT

- In the third week of December the moose start losing their antlers.
- Ptarmigan and wild chicken hunting.
- Travel by dog sleigh.
- Make trails by snowshoe.
- Good time for trapping.
- You can snare rabbits.
- You use up your woodpile, and the kids can play video games by the woodstove. (Um, my dad sent this one in . . .)

- The smoke rises straight up from the chimneys. "That's when you know it's cold: if the smoke is straight up and there is no wind." —Mike Beaver
- "Start your beadwork and sewing for Christmas. Late January and February, days are getting longer after the cold winter months." —Dot Desjarlais

March to April

WHEN THE DAYS GET LONGER:
FIVE MINUTES OF EXTRA SUNSHINE EVERY DAY!

- Caribou camp. Hunt those barren land caribou.
- Ptarmigan hunting.
- Ice fishing (with hooks).
- At the end of March baby wolverines are born.
- Trapping muskrat from March to the end of May before the season closes. —Mike Beaver
- In the old days, men would go to the fort in April and May to sell fur. As the ice melted, they left for the spring beaver and a muskrat hunt. The hunters went from their toboggans to their canoes.
- In April the caribou start migrating to their calving grounds.
- The pregnant caribou cows start to show. They only have a month or so to get to the calving grounds and have their calves.
- "In April, getting the first duck. When they're back from the south. Hang your laundry out

to dry. No dryer sheet can beat the smell of spring!" —Dot Desjarlais
- "Frolics in March!" —Maggie Sikyea and Fred Beaulieu
- "January to March: the moose eat rosebud bushes in the poplar. That's when we hunt moose. The moose do that now. Different eating habits in the season." —Mike Beaver

Please keep in mind that George Jones music is always in season, and a huge mahsi cho to my dad, Jack Van Camp, for providing the bison, buffalo, and wolf information. Thanks, Pops!

***

Look at all the wisdom and insight here gathered with the help of family, friends, heroes, adopted Aunties and Uncles, Elders, Knowledge Keepers, and cultural heroes. Your project and your stories are only stronger when you've gone to those you adore with gifts and payment and permission to share what they know in a good way for you and future generations to enjoy. Mahsi cho to everyone who helped me put this list together.

18.
THE ART OF THE INTRODUCTION

Whenever I head back to Fort Smith, I often have Elders come up to me and say, "Richard Van Camp," but it comes out like this:

"Richard Van CaaaaaaaaAAAAAAAAAAAaaaammmmmmmmmp."

But in actual fact I know what they're up to because I use the same trick.

They are biding their time and checking me out. It's like echolocation meets "Biovoac technology" (I actually don't know what this means, sorry—I just made it up). During this time, they're reading me and my body and my features for info. It's a survival technique.

What they're thinking is, "Holy cow. Did Van Camp pack on the pounds, or what? Look at those little Christmas hams, a.k.a. love handles. Why is his face so puffy? Oh, yup, he has his mother's smile. My my, the hair's receding. Richard Van Camp is proof that your nose and ears never stop growing. My, my, how the years have flown and landed exactly on his face."

Well, maybe I'm exaggerating, but I can sense when someone's checking me out, and I respect that while they're going, "Richard Van Caaaaaaaa-AAAAAAAAAAAAaaaamp," they're gathering intel.

This technique is what you have to hone when you take the stage to start sharing a story. Here are some questions to ask yourself.

1. Is everybody paying attention? Turn that TV off or turn that radio down. Cell phones off? Good.

2. What's the mood? Have the plates been cleared from the table, and has the tea and coffee been poured? Is everyone settled? If you're competing with someone at the end of the table who's talking, calmly and patiently enjoy your tea or coffee and let someone say, "Hey, so and so wants to share a story."

3. What was the story told before? Can you build on it? For example, don't talk real estate right after someone shares a spirit story. Build on the spirit that's in the room.

4. Are people at the table super religious? If so maybe lay off on the "bionic erotic" stories, hey?

5. Is the audience engaged? Yes? Then give 'er. If everyone needs a smoke or a bathroom break, grant it, but know that sharing is a gift—don't waste your knowledge on a room that's not ready or interested or capable of understanding that you're giving pearls out to anyone who's ready.

6. The big question I always ask is: what is the spirit you want to leave everyone with as they head home? A good chuckle? A teaching? A

gentle reminder of how we're all connected? A good ghost story to give everyone the willies? You're in charge here, so be mindful. Stories have power. Stories are power. You're holding a lightning rod of possible emotions that you have a say in, so honour your audience as much as you can because it's always an honour to have someone say, "Can you please share a story with our group before we head home?" or "Can you please share with the group that story you told us that one time when . . . ?"

19.
INTERVIEWING YOUR ELDERS TO RECLAIM A GOOD TEACHING STORY

Rosa Mantla is a Tłı̨chǫ Elder I adore. She's sweet, cheeky, patient, and kind, and I've adopted her as my Tłı̨chǫ aunty. She's helped me work on my comic books, novellas, and short stories every time I ask her to. Every time we get together, we laugh. I'm always recording her for myself and for my family. Here's an interview that I did with Rosa, using my cell phone to videotape her with her permission. I think this shows how interviewing your Elders can lead not only to a good visit and connection but to a very good story, too.

HOW THE WHISKEYJACK AND WOODPECKER TRADED WIVES

RVC = Richard Van Camp
RM = Rosa Mantla

RVC: Rosa, can you tell us about how the Whiskeyjack and the Woodpecker traded wives?

RM: The Whiskeyjack and the Woodpecker.

RVC: Oh, yes.

RM: I heard this story the first time when we took the boys out on a camp. It was way out on the winter road but further out in the bushy wooded area. Early one morning, when we were eating in a tent with the boys, my husband, Henri Pierre Mantla, looked outside. As he saw the birds, he asked to open the tent flap more because it was hot inside. And the whiskeyjacks were outside looking for food. And we had scraps of meat left for the birds or other animals. Whiskeyjack was already helping himself, eating. Then, all of a sudden, my husband said, "It is said that the Whiskeyjack and the Woodpecker traded wives long ago."

And the Whiskeyjack had a nice and cheerful and fat wife that the Woodpecker admired. And the Woodpecker was always nearby pecking on a tree, every day. And then one day, the Woodpecker asked the Whiskeyjack, "Can we trade wives? Can I trade my wife with you?" And the Whiskeyjack said, "Why? I don't want to trade my wife for another wife." And the Woodpecker said, "I would like to trade my wife with you." The Whiskeyjack said, "How can you feed my wife when I feed her fat and meat every day? That's why she is so nice looking." So he said, "I can't give you my wife, because she is going to starve." The Woodpecker said, "No, no, no. My wife lives with me. She is not starving." But the Whiskeyjack said, "How can you feed my wife when all you do is pick on the wood every day, and this is what you use for food?" And the Woodpecker said, "No, no. I will take care of her. I will feed her well. And she will be surviving with me." The Whiskeyjack said, "No, I can't do it. I can't."

But the next day the Woodpecker put pressure on him again, so Whiskeyjack said, "Okay. Make sure you look after my wife and you have to feed her well." And the Woodpecker said, "Oh, yes. I will. I will feed her what you feed her: fat and meat."

So they traded wives. A couple of months later, Whiskeyjack saw the Woodpecker on the tree all by himself at times, so many times that finally he asked him, "What did you do to my wife?"

Woodpecker kept on pecking on the tree.

"What did you do to my wife?" Whiskeyjack said again.

And [Woodpecker] didn't say nothing, so, "My wife died because you didn't feed her the food that she usually eats, huh? I smother her with fatty food, but my wife died of starvation?"

And the Woodpecker said, "Yes. She couldn't eat the bits of pieces from the wood, even wood worms, so she died."

So the Whiskeyjack was so mad and angry that he said, "Whatever you are meant to be eating, that is your food. My wife doesn't live on the bits of pieces of wood and worms that you peck on every day. So from now on, you will always live the way you were brought up into this world, pecking on the wood, digging for worms."

RVC: Mahsi cho.

RM: So as we were talking about this story later on, there's always examples from the animals and birds—

that they have lived and how they have experience in their lifetime. So my husband said, "Maybe this is the reason why we have so many people kind of living in different relationships. And sometimes they are not prepared, they don't plan it, and they don't have the skills to adapt to different changes. So some relationships work; some don't. Just like the Woodpecker lives on the tree bits and worms as he pecks them; whereas the Whiskeyjack would gather food, meat, fish, any food, but not garbage."

RVC: Mahsi cho. Thanks, Rosa.

RM: You're welcome.

***

I think this is such a good story—we love hearing stories of animals and relationships. We love resolutions and morals. But we also just love the pure entertainment and the joy of listening, not knowing where the storyteller is taking us.

So your homework now is to interview an Elder whom you adore—and who grants permission—and bring back a story—again, if you have permission!— that you and the Elder may be worried the world will forget. Don't wait. Then make copies for the Elder's family and for your own. Pay this Elder and feed them. Bring them food. Bring them groceries. Spoil them. Visit them. Call them. Check in on them. You owe them so much now and always.

20.
WHAT STORY DO YOU NEED FOR PEACE?

'**ve always wondered about our family. Why weren't we taught our language? Why were we raised in Fort Smith and not Behchokǫ̀ where my mom, Rosa Wah-Shee, was born and my grandparents and cousins and aunties and uncles lived? Don't get me wrong—Fort Smith will always be my hometown, and I love it so much, but there was always this quiet question inside of me: why was my mom taken from her parents when she was five years old and, for the next twelve years of her life, why did she have to go to two different residential schools in Fort Smith—Breynat Hall and Grandin College?

Keep in mind, my mother was one of 100,000 or more children who were taken away from their parents for the purpose of killing the Indian in the child. Stories destroy too—or can—so you need to be careful of the stories you tell. The church and the government told Indigenous people that we were wrong, less than, and that we needed to change. Don't believe me? This is what Bishop Grandin himself wrote in 1875 about Indigenous Peoples: "We instil in them a pronounced distaste for the Native life so that they will be humiliated when reminded of their origins. When they graduate from our institutions, the children have lost everything Native except their blood."

Through our stories and traditions and languages, we are reclaiming ourselves, coming together, gathering, and gaining strength through our love and connection—remembering and recalling our stories and passing them on for medicine and strength and love and healing.

When I look back on my life, it was my parents, friends, and Fort Smith family and Elders who took me under their wings, and it was these cultural guardians who gave me my Northern culture. I am Fort Smith in heart and in spirit, but the sense that we were part of cultural genocide has never left me, and this is why I write. This is why I share stories. This is why I record my Elders: so I can help others who are looking for their cultures, too.

This journey of mine to curate stories for *Gather* gave me the courage to finally ask my mom the one question I'd always wanted to ask for the one story I needed as a father, husband, son, and brother: "Was residential school a good experience?" I wanted to hear from my mother what it was like the first night that she was away from her parents.

MY INTERVIEW WITH MY MOTHER, ROSA WAH-SHEE, ABOUT HER RESIDENTIAL SCHOOL EXPERIENCE

RICHARD: Mom, was residential school a good experience? What do you remember from being a little girl? How old were you?

M: According to the records, I was five. I was not supposed to be going to school that year, but because my brothers ran into the house and said that they were packing to go to school, I said, "I want to go to school, too, because I don't want to be left behind again."

They said, "Then grab a suitcase."

"What do I put in it?"

"All your clothes. But your name isn't on the list," they said.

"You two can put me on the list."

"We can't put you on the list."

"Why do you need me on the list?"

"You can't get on the bus if your name's not on the list."

I said, "Then YOU get me on the bus without my name on the list."

We went running up the hill with our suitcases in hand from the house and joined other children standing in a crowd as names were being called out by an Indian Agent. Children got into the bus as their names were called. Finally, both my brothers' names were called. I walked between both my brothers towards the bus, and they wedged me between them as we took steps into the bus while the Indian Agent continued to call out names. That's how I got into the bus!

As I looked out the window of the bus, I saw the Indian Agent still calling names, children walking into the bus and finding seats. Parents were gathering towards the bus, tapping the windows to talk to their children on the bus, others reaching to get near the bus, all in tears, and some waving good-byes. Then I saw my parents. Mom and dad managed to get to our window, crying and telling my brothers to look after me and not to leave me alone. I have never seen my parents cry before.

I had never been on a bus ride before. It was Autumn and the leaves were turning colours along the dirt road to Yellowknife. It was a dusty bus ride, our faces, hair and clothing were coated with dust when we arrived at the Yellowknife airport, where we were all transported to what looked like a huge, black World War II airplane. There were only a few seats on the plane, so children had to sit on the floor or stand alongside this plane during the flight. I had never been in one place where there were only children. There were children that I have never seen before. They came from all the Tłįchǫ communities: Yellowknife, Fort Resolution, Hay River, and other communities. We were like sardines in this huge airplane. Then we went into the air on this plane. Most of us have never been on a plane in our lives. I had my first bleeding nose on the airplane. I was in the clouds for the first time in my life. Then I realized, this was not a game. This plane was taking me away to an unknown distance from home. With all the land and lakes below from the air that the plane was passing, I knew it was not possible to make it back home.

I didn't know the world was much bigger than my home community of Fort Rae until I saw the land base and the lakes below from the plane. I thought we were just a universe of our own, that Fort Rae existed in a dome. Then we landed in Fort Smith. They had streets, while we had trails to houses and tents back home. There were fences around homes, two storey houses with big windows, and tall and huge buildings that were bigger than our log houses. We learned later that one big building was the school, and even bigger than that was a three-storey brick building next to it where we would all live. There were lawns, yards, green grass all the same length, roads were very wide, made out of small rocks, and cars and trucks driving on these roads.

We were told to get out of the bus and to get into four groups based on our sizes. Once we got into four groups, they separated us into junior boys and girls and senior boys and girls as we stood on the lawn outside what was called Breynat Hall. I looked at our group of little girls and realized I did not know most of the other girls except those that came from our community. I looked for my brothers, and they were standing with the other senior boys. There were sixty junior boys and girls and thirty senior boys and girls.

There were only nuns and priests facing us as we stood on the lawn in our groups. I had no idea what was being said and I just watched hand gestures of the priest speaking and his expressions. I had only seen priests and nuns in church and the hospital. Then as they moved towards the different groups, I noticed my brothers were starting to move away from our group along with the other boys towards the huge brick building. I panicked and yelled, "Mom and Dad said you are not supposed to leave me!" I did not want to be separated from my brothers and I tried to run to them. Then my brother James said, "We will be right back." They did not return to get me, and we never spoke to each other again. We remained separated though we lived in the same building.

Whenever we were all in the cafeteria, lined up for meals in our separate groups, we could not speak to each other. That included if we were lined up beside each other. If we tried to greet each other and did, we were punished. We had to always remain with our group. We had to sit separately from each other during meals and with our group. We could only see each other from the distance and across the room.

Everything was happening so fast. Our group of little girls were taken into a big room in this huge building. The nuns lined us up and we took turns sitting on a chair to have our hair cut. Many girls cried as they saw their hair falling to the floor; so did I. We all started to look the same. Then they give us clothes and a number that would be ours. They told us to take our clothes off and get into a little space after putting on a cover over our chest and a little skirt. Then they turned water on us. I have never been in a shower before and water was coming out of the walls and draining into the floor. I found it strange to watch water gushing out of the walls. I did not understand how this could happen. They told us to put our hands out and they put a liquid into our hands and made gestures to wash our hair with it. They gave us towels to dry ourselves and told us to put on the clothes with our numbers sewn on them and to put our clothes we had worn into our suitcases and put them on top of the lockers. Our numbers they gave us were sewn on every clothing we had: the smock, the jeans, even the socks they gave us to wear and our shoes.

We went into a dorm of sixty beds, thirty beds in each dorm. We just picked the bed we wanted to sleep on. They gave us a toothbrush, toothpaste, combs, and pjs. We kept our new clothes given to us together in a small shelf unit with our number on it. That was the beginning of our new life.

As we were all putting our suitcases away, I asked an older girl next to me in Dogrib, "When are we going home?" She answered in another language I did not understand. I gathered she had learned English and had been to school before. So, I asked her in Dogrib,

"In which season will we go home?" She said, "In the summer." It was Fall. Now I knew we were not going home for a very long time.

The nights were grieving times. A time of remembering, picking, and eating fresh berries, having fish and bannock, including beaver and muskrats, going for boat rides, playing with friends all day, visiting relatives, Mom braiding my hair every day, attending tea dances and handgames, sleeping with our parents and holding Mom around the waist during the nights as I slept next to her. Thoughts of winter brought memories of when the jingle of bells around the sled dogs' harnesses would tell us my older brothers and Dad were returning from a caribou hunt and trapping! We would leap out of our beds in the middle of the night to greet them. Then we would have a feast of fresh-cooked caribou meat and bone marrow in the middle of the night. Those happy days were gone. I would hear other girls crying in bed during the nights and that would make me very sad and cry, too.

The food served was very different from our traditional food. We were served food we had never eaten before. There were times the food smelled really sweet. I could not eat spinach. It reminded me of frogs. I would gag and the nun would stand behind me and would not leave until I put the spinach in my mouth and drank a full glass of milk to swallow it. One day, I thought we were having blood soup. I was so happy! But it tasted so sweet that I started to gag. It was tomato soup.

Every morning we had to do chores and our work had to be inspected before we went to school. All beds had to be made properly, and they had to be in straight rows. The mirrors, sinks, taps, and toilets had to be cleaned. The floors had to be swept with a dry mop, and on weekends the hallway between the two dorms had to be polished.

At first, none of us knew where to go in the big school. I did not know how to read, so I was led around until they took me to a classroom and told me to sit at a desk. One day, the nun who was our teacher came over to my desk and quietly asked what was my name? I did not understand her. She made a hand gesture to say her name. I then said my Indian name, Ts'èkoa, which was Little Girl. She said, "No, no, no, no—English name." She said she would find out my name. I thought, "How is she going to find out?" I was told by my mother that my grandmother had delivered me on the beach and nobody else was there, so how will she find out my name? The nun came to me the next day, leaned over me, and quietly said that my name was Rosa Wah-Shee. She wrote this name on a piece of paper and put it on my desk. I asked, "Who told you?" She said, "The Bishop." I asked, "How does he know?" She said, "He's got a big book." I said, "Bishop wasn't there when I was born." I didn't understand.

The only big book we ever heard about was from going to church every day. We prayed and sang in Latin. In the evenings we had rosaries. The big book was when after you died: St. Peter and God would open this big book to see if you had been good while on Earth. If you were, then you went to heaven. Nobody told us that Bishop also had a big book and that he knew when we were all born and what our name was in English.

It is true that we were programmed. We were absolutely programmed every day. We prayed so much: we prayed before breakfast; we prayed in the evening after dinner, and then we prayed by our bedside every night. We also went to high mass on Sundays, all dressed the same in white and black, and took all the front pews. We prayed, prayed, and prayed all the time. They even gave us confession days. It would get difficult to try and remember doing anything wrong from week to week. It would get to a point where we would worry about it amongst ourselves and would start making up sins we had committed. But then, we also did not want to repeat a sin we said we committed last week in case the priest would remember them! Yet we also did not want to stay too short a time in the confession room either, as we were all being watched by our supervisors who were nuns. The only time I remembered praying so hard after supper was when I wanted us to have permission to finish our soccer game after our rosary, because we had a tie game and I wanted our team to win the game. I could not believe it when my prayer was answered!!

We were told we had to learn to read and write in English by Christmas. We were not allowed to speak in our language. If any girl got caught speaking their language, they were punished in front of the other girls. They were slapped and had their hair pulled by the nuns. It was so terrifying to watch how mean the nuns could be to the girls, and hearing these girls cry out in pain each time was unbearable. We had no one to protect us.

I think my goal to be able to speak and write in English was to preserve and protect myself from the nuns. It seemed to me that the nuns constantly looked for trouble. To blame any girl for the least little thing. Waiting for any girl to do something wrong, to scold somebody, to slap and to hit them! If a girl lost something coming out of the laundry, which wasn't their fault, they still had reason to beat that girl. They would say for example, "Find your sock!" The girl can never find that sock no matter if they looked in the playroom or in the dormitory because the sock got lost in the laundry room where women in the community worked to wash our clothes.

My life went into self-protection. I knew I had nobody to protect me from the nuns. There might be sixty girls, but nobody else is going to help you. The nuns did not help us with our homework, nor did they volunteer to do so. They spoke in French most of the time to each other and when they were around us. I chose to study and complete my homework in the cafeteria after supper every weeknight with the senior students because that was an option we had, so I took it to stay out of trouble with the nuns. Within three months I was reading and writing in English.

Our supervisor would stack our report cards and call out each girl and read out their marks aloud so all the other little girls could hear. If they did poorly, the nun would say they are so dumb and retarded that they were given a balloon to play with as they sat on the floor in front of all the other little girls. These girls would cry as they played with the balloon. Most of the girls that did poorly in school never returned after they entered their teenage years. Their parents took them out on the land before they were to return to residential school in the Fall.

When we returned home for the summer, we returned to our language, culture, and belief systems. We could speak our language freely once again and take part in our cultural systems. Though the communities lost so many children every year to the residential school system, the communities continued to thrive as it always did. It was always exciting to be home, to be with family and relatives again. We did not have running water or electricity then, but it was great to help my mother clean the house, wash clothes, and hang them outside to dry. Mom and Dad would take us to where they used to camp when we were kids. This brought our family together. Mom would cook fish, beaver, muskrats, and bannock and serve them over a table cloth on spruce bows in the tent like we use too. We always lived close to water when I was growing up and being back by the water always brought great memories of my childhood.

I had ten brothers, and I am the only girl in the family. Most of my brothers went to residential school. Some went to the same residences, and I know most have had traumatic experiences. They never talked to me about it. But it is their story. My brothers and I have respect for each other, but the residential school stole the close kinship we had as a family before we were separated to attend residential school.

That is some of my experiences at Breynat Hall in Fort Smith.

R: Do you remember your number?

M: Twelve.

R: Oh, twelve years.

M: Yup.

R: Breynat Hall you went to first? And then Grandin.

M: Yes, then I entered Grandin College when I started grade seven with other junior high and high school students. There were fourteen of us girls the first year. I later graduated from there.

R: You went to Grandin in grade seven, wow! Thank you, Mom. That was . . .

I actually had no words. I was just so proud of my mom and her brothers and my grandparents for the courage they all had to summon, I am sure, one second at a time after the children were taken away.

***

I have always said that residential schools will always be the sorrow in Canada's bones, and I send my absolute respect to all survivors and their families. To those who made it home and to those who didn't.

It will take generations to come out of the shadows of residential schools and the legacy of extinguishment we've all survived. Think about forced sterilization, the '60s Scoop, day schools, residential schools, and every peaceful demonstration brutalized by police for Indigenous Peoples standing up for their rights.

What's the old saying? It takes resource extraction to make profits. Indigenous people who know their rights and have the backing of supreme court rulings are often "in the way" of "progress." Bring in the police and workers who have no relation to the land, the people, or the history and who do not know about these supreme court rulings, and we have more fighting.

And now you know why so many of us are dedicating our lives to reclaiming our stories, our songs, our prayers, our languages, our relationships with the land, our ceremonies, our traditions, our offerings, our families, our societies, our clans, our obligations, and ourselves.

21.
CONTEMPORARY INDIGENOUS STORYTELLING AND HONOURING THE LATE TREVOR EVANS WITH STORIES

I want to talk a little about contemporary Indigenous storytelling. A long time ago—maybe, thirty-five years ago—I was sitting around a campfire with the great and late Trevor Evans. And I want to dedicate this story to his parents, Earl and Marlene Evans, whom I love with everything inside of me. I also want to dedicate this story to Trevor's children: Trey, Elle, and Chance Diamond.

Trevor and I were sitting around a fire, might have been Tsu Lake or winter camp, and he told us this story I never forgot. You know Trevor was always wise beyond his years, and I really want to honour him today with this story.

So he said, "You guys ever hear that story about that old bull moose making his way through a blizzard?"

And we all looked at him. We didn't know if it was going to be a joke, and we said, "No."

He said, "I never told you that story?"

I said, "No."

He says, "Okay," he says, "get ready."

A long time ago, this old bull moose was lost in a blizzard, and he was making his way, and the way the snow had thawed and froze again, it was really sharp that top layer—was really sharp on his knees and legs. He was getting really tired, and he sent out a little prayer for help, and he was getting really weary. He was getting bone weary, and all of a sudden he saw this big tipi in the field and nice smoke coming up, and it looked so nice and warm in there. He started making his way to this big tipi. As he got closer, he peeked in and there were these two young bull moose—they were sitting in that tipi. They were warming themselves by that fire, and there was food.

"Come in," they said. "Come in, Uncle. Warm yourself."

"Oh, man," he said. He went right in that tipi. He shut that flap, so those moose are in there and they're warming themselves, eating, and then they started talking about the fall and their hopes for the spring, and as they were talking, this Pipe came in through the door. It floated, this Pipe. And right away those young bull moose got scared.

"Oh no!" They said, "Don't touch it! Don't! Don't! Whatever you do, don't touch it!"

And here that old bull moose, he grabbed that Pipe. He took a big puff, and he went, *phewww*. He let the smoke out. And then he let that Pipe go, and that Pipe floated outside the door and went back out into the night, back into that blizzard.

"Oh no," they said. "Uh-oh. We told you not to touch that Pipe. Any moose that touches that Pipe, they don't live long."

He said, "That's okay," he said.

He says, "I was hungry, but now I'm full. I was cold, but now I'm warm. It's good," he said. "Let's go to sleep. Tomorrow is a brand-new day," he said.

The younger moose, they just shook their heads at him, and they all laid down and went to bed.

In the morning they ate a little bit more, they made sure that the fire was out, and they started going out of the tipi. And the two bull moose, the younger ones, they started going one way, and that old bull moose started going the other way, and he was returning to his homeland. And as he was walking, this arrow came and got him right in the heart, we'll say—right here. And that bull moose went down, that big one. And the two young ones came, and they said, "We told you not to touch that Pipe. Anyone who touches that Pipe and they blow into it—they give it back, they don't live long. We told you not to touch it, and here you touched it and now you're not going to see the sunset tonight."

And that old one looked at them. He said, "That Pipe is a hunter's prayer. That Pipe is a hunter who is living a good life, is hunting for the people, and it's good," he says.

"They're honouring the Treaty. They've lived in a good way. His family has lived in a good way," he says. "I'm gonna live forever now. In the laughter of their children and their grandchildren and their grandchildren's grandchildren. That's the Treaty we have with the humans, and they're not going to waste anything. They know what to do with the meat and the sinew and my fur and my bones. I'm going to live forever now. That's why we smoke that Pipe. That's the breath of life that we share together."

***

And so Trevor told us that story. I just never forgot that, and I thought, boy, that man really knows his stuff. And the other day, a couple days ago, we were telling stories down in the river valley in Edmonton by the fire, and I told that story to some friends, and it hit me halfway through that, well, they're vegetarians. So maybe this story doesn't apply to them, but the good news about storytelling is there are some stories that are meant to be added onto. Not changed—they are meant to be honoured and adopted.

So I said:

> And for all you vegetarians out there, you can always change the story next time you are camping. You can say, "A long time ago, there was this old carrot, and he was just rolling his way through the storm, and he came upon this tipi, and there are two young carrots in there and they had a nice fire, and there was soil and vitamins for that soil; and they just sat around telling good stories." And then you can still have that Pipe—and an old Pipe comes in, and those two carrots, they backed up.
>
> "Oh, oh, oh," they said as a warning. And that old carrot partook in the breath of life that we all share together, and he smoked that Pipe.

You can modify it so it's that way. Then you can say, "The next day, that old Carrot rolls out, and he's picked up into the sky, and those young ones say, 'Hey! We told you not to touch that Pipe!'"

That old Carrot can look down and say, "That is the gardener's prayer. That gardener is living a good life. There's no chemicals. Everyone's happy. I'm gonna live forever in the laughter of their children, their grandchildren, and their grandchildren's grandchildren."

So I wanted to share that with you today to honour the great and late Trevor Evans.

I really miss his storytelling. I don't know where he got that story: maybe from his dad, Earl, or Kenny Hudson, or his grandpa—I don't know, but I wanted to share that story about my dear friend who passed three years ago now. I miss him every day.

When we share stories about our loved ones who have passed, we travel their stories forward, and I like to think they're smiling in the spirit world, knowing their children are hearing their stories maybe for for the first time, maybe for the hundredth time, but each time it is a loving blanket placed upon them and that, I think, is the medicine of stories.

* * *

I posted this story on my YouTube channel. If you want to see and hear me share it, you'll see how I pace it, how my voice changes. I did tweak it here for the printed version, and I do dedicate this to Trevor's family and to his memory.

And now I want to give you some homework. Go back in time and get the story you've wanted like I did with my good friend Trevor Evans. For instance, there was another really good one that Trevor Evans told me. I will not tell it here, but this story is that of "the haunted woodstove of Fort Smith." It is the one story that always terrified me—besides the Goat Man—all about a woodstove and a haunting that visited Fort Smith in the 1970s. I'd beg Trevor to tell it when we were camping, and I'd stay awake so scared to even breathe long after Trevor had fallen asleep. I've told and retold this story so many times, but I could never do it justice the way Trevor told it. I nagged him for years and years to let me record him sharing this account of a visit with a haunted woodstove. I wanted to record it so I could always have the story in his own words, and I wanted to transcribe it for him. Lucky for me, his appendix blew, and he was laid up at the Stanton Regional Hospital in Yellowknife. I seized my chance. Trevor was nineteen years old then. When I asked Trevor to tell the story, he asked, "Do you want me to spruce it up?" "No!" I said, "Just tell it the way you've always told it. It's amazing enough." And though I won't tell it here, I want you to go get all those scary campfire stories and be sure to pass them on because we also like to be scared—well, some of us—but it's so that we can learn to overcome the fear, too, maybe. And here is the real treasure for me of the haunted wood stove story: Trevor passed at the tender age of forty-three, but I had this story and I had this recording. I was able to convert it to MP3 and mail it to all his friends, family, and children who were hurting after he passed. I'm grateful that I have all the tapes we made for each other. Indeed, in 1989, when I was seventeen and Trev was fifteen, we recorded ourselves singing, talking, recounting, reading Iron Maiden lyrics, gossiping, and playing our favourite tunes. I have this one recording of Trev singing "Hard Luck Woman." Man, there was nothing Trevor Evans couldn't do. Thank goodness we took the time to do this for one another. And his children and his parents and his friends and I will always have these memories. Mahsi cho and with respect to Trevor Evans's family.

22.
THE CIRCLE OF LIFE

Years ago I was invited to Spearfish, South Dakota. There I met a Lakota Elder who won my heart with her sincerity, cheekiness, and love of life and laughter. Every chance I had to visit with Jace DeCory, I did. She reminded me of our own Elders in Fort Smith: Irene Sanderson, Rosa Mercredi, Seraphine Evans, and Dora Tourangeau to name a few.

As we visited through the years, Jace told me a story over a supper one night that made my jaw drop. In preparing this book of medicine for you, I asked Jace if she could write down the story she had told me, and she has. Mahsi cho, Jace. I am grateful.

* * *

"Grandpa Frank Fools Crow, respected Oglala Lakota medicine man and spiritual leader, now in the Spirit World, once described me to my future husband, Sam.

Grandpa said that Sam, he would meet a woman with long dark hair who wore glasses and we would be re-united again in this life. You see, we had been together many, many years ago in another time.

I first met my husband, Sam, while we were at a Lakota language conference which was held in Pierre, South Dakota, our state capitol. It was 1979. It was amazing to see all of these Lakota people conversing and giving presentations in the Lakota language only. Little, if any, English was spoken.

English is my first language and, as a young Lakota woman, I sort of felt left out as the Elders talked, but I continued to listen intently because our language sounded so beautiful. Many of our relatives had grown up speaking Lakota, but they had lost much of it during the boarding school days.

As I struggled to understand a Lakota word every now and then, I felt blessed because seated to my left was my mother, Dorothy, and to my right was my Aunt Nellie. Both were fluent in Lakota, and they served as my informal Lakota "translators." The people were joyous that day—talking and laughing with the won-derful sounds of the Lakota language, and the people all around us.

That afternoon I noticed a Lakota man, sort of a cowboy-looking fellow, long braid, with the words "Isnala Wakan Inajin" tooled on his leather belt. I asked my Ina (mom) what that meant, and she replied, "Stand-ing Alone Holy." I was intrigued by these words and I guessed that this was his Lakota name. Later that evening at dinner, a cousin introduced me to this man. We met face to face that evening, but I felt that I already knew him. I had seen this man before, but where and when? As we continued our visit into the night, we briefly shared our life stories, but when we began to speak of sacred ceremony, my heart began to pound.

In the mid-1960s I was embarking on a way of life that I had only visited with my Unci [grandmother] Scholastica Mad Bear about as I was growing up. In the early 1970s, after graduating from college, this world that my Unci had initially introduced me to was starting to unfold. I began my spiritual journey which I continue to walk today . . . the way of the Cannupa, the Sacred Pipe, and the Lakota ceremonies that go along with this spiritual path, including the most sacred Sun Dance.

But back to Sam. As we visited, as Sam talked, I found myself finishing his words. I knew what he was going to say before he said it. We talked about commitment to this way of life, of Sweat Lodges and the Sun Dance and Grandpa Fools Crow's love of the people. I talked about my times at Sun Dances with a number of Lakota Elders at Green Grass on the Cheyenne River Reservation. In the 1970s we referred to it as the "International Sun Dance," because there were people from all over the Lakota Nation and beyond who danced there. I felt fortunate to be at these sacred ceremonies with Sun Dance Chief Grandpa Frank Fools Crow and other respected Lakota spiritual leaders, including Pete Catches, John Fire, and Henry and Leonard Crow Dog, to name a few. I told Sam how I was so full of emotion during those early days. Also that I needed to learn and experience more teachings before I made my decision to carry a Cannupa and commit to these seven sacred ceremonies of the Pipe Way, the traditional ways of my people. Would I have the faith, strength, and heart to live this way?

But back to Sam: on one hot mid-August day in Green Grass, there were many dancers who gave of themselves, who sacrificed so that we may live. As the sun was getting closer to Maka, the earth, three male dancers were staked to the ground, prepared to stay all night pierced to the Sacred Tree. What commitment, I thought. Would they be able to fulfill their vows? And each man had only a thin star quilt for a night that could turn cold.

I could not get these three men out of my head. Tossing and turning, I finally woke up a younger relative, Jackie, and I asked her to accompany me to the circle to maybe give some support to these three men who were praying for who knows what, but certainly for something very important. We slipped on our winter jackets because it was indeed a cold summer night. We each took an extra blanket along to sit on under the Sun Dance arbor. As we looked upon these three dark, covered, visibly shivering men, we both felt instantly ashamed. Here we were there to lend our prayers in support, but we were warm and comfortable, and we were not suffering. Jackie went back to the tent to retrieve one more blanket, and upon her return, we handed them to a helper who was near the arbor, and he took the three blankets to these dancers. We felt better. Maybe they did, too?

As we prayed that evening, many wonderful things were revealed to us. The prayers from these men must have been very strong, because the little lights that emanated from their bodies jumped from their piercing ropes to the top of the rustling cottonwood leaves. It was kind of like Christmas lights in summer and it made us feel happy and loved. As we watched and prayed, we saw something in the sky moving slowly—a bright shining star? A meteor or an airplane? Or airships form some other place? Whatever it was, it was moving ever so slowly over our heads. And then, all of a sudden, it vanished; it was gone. Grandpa Fools Crow used to talk of other Nations and living beings in other worlds. He always reminded us not to be afraid of these things, as they were just as curious about us, especially about us Natives, the Lakota people.

There were many powerful things that happened at that particular Sun Dance in 1972 and in many more to come. But I have shared these experiences with only a few other close relatives. I held these teachings close to my heart.

Back to visiting with Sam. As we continued to visit, I felt that I could share some of these happenings with this man, Sam. I trusted him because he was also a Sun Dancer, he walked the Pipe Way, and he was close to Grandpa Fools Crow. We shared how much respect and love we had for this Oglala Lakota spiritual leader. At that time, Sam was even staying with Grandpa Frank and Grandma Kate, out in the country near Kyle, on the Pine Ridge Indian Reservation.

Then I said to Sam, "I'll bet you have never been at a Sun Dance where there were visitors from outer space?" He looked at me incredulously and said, "I'll bet I have!" He said that he, too, had seen the "spaceship," along with his fellow fasters. Perhaps the six of us who prayed near the Sacred Tree that night had all experienced something very special. Sam then spoke of the time when he and his brothers, Mel and Avery, were staked to the Tree and it was so very cold, but a young woman and a younger girl brought them blankets. "Was it you?" Sam asked. I think he knew the answer. I told Sam that it was indeed me and my cousin Jackie who were there to help support them, and we did indeed send in the extra blankets. "We didn't know who you all were, but it was cold, and we felt sad for you," I replied. Sam thanked me that evening in Pierre and told me that they were able to finish their commitment because we took pity on them that night. We both agreed that this is what we grew up with, the teachings of our Lakota Elders, to live with compassion. And little did I know that the man I prayed for would one day be my husband and the father of our two sons, Junior and Dawson.

That cold night, the stars in the sky and the shiny bright objects in the tree and in the heavens brought us together. It was meant to be, so said Grandpa Fools Crow. And so it was, and is.

Jace DeCory, Lakota (Cheyenne River Sioux Tribe)
Assistant Professor, American Indian Studies
College of Liberal Arts
Black Hills State University
Spearfish, South Dakota

THE CHEAT SHEET!

23.
THE CHEAT SHEET! A.K.A. UNCLE RICHARD VAN CAMP'S STORYTELLING TIPS

One of our Dene laws is to share stories every day.

I am lucky to tour as an author and storyteller, and I find that when I'm marketed as a writer visiting a community, we can sometimes pack the room, but when I'm marketed as a storyteller, it's standing room only. I think this is because we are all lonesome for stories; we are all lonesome for connection and community. It's stories that unite us and remind us of our place in the world as brothers and sisters, and it's an honour to be known as a great storyteller.

I wanted to sit down and share a few tips on how anyone can become a great storyteller. For those who are nervous as a public speaker, there's an old storyteller's trick where you bring a lot of props, so this way you can hide behind them for a bit before the spirit of the stories you wish to share gets everyone in the room sharing.

There's also another great technique where you get everyone in the room to introduce themselves; ask them why they've come and, chances are, your visitors will get going on their own stories, and that'll spark the room. Really, it's just great practice as a visitor, a guest, and a host to always have a story ready.

Everyone loves a great ghost story and a sweet love story, and I'll share a couple more of these here! And everyone loves hearing about how someone beat the unbeatable. Remember Rocky? What's your story of triumph, either from your own life, your family, or your culture? Start writing it, and speaking it, and practicing it. I bet you can amaze someone if you share it.

And I'll help you get started with my tips provided here. I hope my pointers help you out. Some I've already shared, but repetition is key with learning and storytelling.

STORYTELLING TIP #1: LOCATE YOURSELF AND HONOUR YOUR AUDIENCE

Here's the good news: all great storytelling sessions are really just a great opportunity to visit.

A great storyteller leaves his or her audience better than he or she found them, so if you go into a room with a closed mind about what stories you are going to tell, you may be missing out on a chance to really connect with your listeners.

It is very important that when you do go before an audience you first locate yourself. Please tell people who you are and where you are from. It is always respectful to acknowledge the traditional people of the land on whose territory you are standing. For example, a great way to say this is, "I would like to acknowledge the Musqueam people on whose traditional territory we are gathered here today." If you do not know whose land you are on, you can say, "I would like to acknowledge the traditional keepers of this territory on whose land we gather today." This way you acknowledge the traditional people of the land and the Ancestors and the land itself.

Without these introductions of who you are and where you are from, the bond will not have begun properly for a good visit. I have seen many times a story-teller who launches into stories that are fantastic but ruined because the audience does not know who this person is or where they are from or why this storyteller should be trusted.

Everyone likes to learn, and when you introduce yourself, you are extending the hand of friendship, and that is storytelling in a good way.

What I like to do is go into a room, thank my hosts, acknowledge whose traditional territory we are gathered on, tell people where I am from, and share some stories about Fort Smith and my family and being raised in a time of storytelling and visiting. The whole time I am doing this, I am reading the audience to see if there are any children or youth who may be nervous if I tell adult stories or stories that are about ghosts or bad medicine. Believe me, if you're going to make children nervous, you are going to have parents nervous, and that shouldn't be the case. Your audience should be engaged and curious as to what you are going to say, not dreading another story that is offensive to the values of those who have travelled to see you.

So locate yourself and then read your audience, see who you are speaking to, and all the while you should be sensing what is acceptable and what isn't with your audience. Also, if you are sensing that the audience is getting tired, it is always wise to cut your presentation short.

The key here is to connect to your audience through eye contact, voice level, body language, and sincerity. Go on out there and have fun. Storytelling is just like dancing or swimming—you've got to get on out there and give 'er!

It's so easy: locate, read, eye contact—they now know you and you know them. Connection is established from the start! And now be real and present.

STORYTELLING TIP #2: BE THERE

There is nothing more important than being completely centered when you are about to share some good medicine with a group. Yes, we all have struggles. Everybody has problems. But you have to let that all go when you walk into a room.

A group will know if you are not completely there. Humans can sense worry and distraction in other humans. It's a survival thing. Can they trust you if you are looking over your shoulder and stammering your way through a half-hearted attempt at a story? Probably not.

Please know that when you stand up to share a story, people are automatically rooting for you. People want to visit. People *need* to visit! We are social animals, just like wolves!

As a storyteller, all you have to do is be there, enjoy yourself, share what it is you need to share, and you'll be surprised how easy it is to really celebrate being alive in front of your listeners.

Honour them!

STORYTELLING TIP #3: DON'T SCOLD OR LECTURE

This is important. I've gone to many storytelling conferences and still wince when I think of the storytellers who have stood up and scolded their audience for not living a certain way or lecturing them on why their way of life is better than anyone else's. Yikes! This is not a good way, in my opinion, to honour anyone.

And it only shows that storytellers who do that are pushing an agenda and that is not honouring your audience because, as a storyteller, you are there to honour the people who have travelled to see you and learn something from you.

By walking into a room with an agenda, you have already closed off that crucial human connection that we are all wishing to feel with one another. People will sense it right away, and you will only bring a room down fast.

No single person has a monopoly on a better way of life. Every nation has something to offer us in the circle of life.

Those who have shown up to listen to you want to learn something, want to feel something, want to laugh, and want to let go. They have made the time for you and do not need to be scolded or be made to feel less than they are.

Honour your audience. Uplift their spirits. A great storyteller leaves each place better than they found it.

A ho!

STORYTELLING TIP #4: LET GO

A great storytelling session is a dance of trust. Your audience is trusting you to take them to places of mystery and joy—a place they have not been—and you have to trust your audience to guide you so that you can do exactly this.

This involves letting go.

Many times when I walk into a room or lecture hall I have no idea what stories I am going to share. It could be about the haunted wood stove in Fort Smith; it could be about the traditional medicine used in our town; it could even be about growing up in the Hickey and Nickname Capital of Canada. As I'm talking, I'm gauging the crowd and sensing what our honoured guests need for a great storytelling session.

As I locate myself in front of an audience and share a bit about my background in terms of family, hometown, and where I work, I establish that crucial bridge between myself and the audience. I am surveying the audience and feeling my way through the energy in the room.

Many times I share a story and have no idea why I am sharing it. I am completely into it and am quietly thinking, "Oh Richard. Richard, Richard, Richard. Why are you sharing a ghost story so soon?"

Many times after a great visit with an audience, I have people thanking me so much for sharing a certain story. "I really needed to hear that story you told. It was good medicine for me." And that's that.

You see, I did not guide the audience. I located myself, got a sense of the energy in the room, opened my heart and mind and then let the audience guide me in what stories they wanted to hear.

So when you walk into a room and begin your visit, let go and begin the dance of trust.

Your listeners will love you for it!

STORYTELLING TIP #5: FIND A MENTOR OR MENTORS

One of the best things a storyteller at any level can do is surround themselves with storytellers they admire. The more we listen and observe, the more tricks of the trade we can adopt. Imitate those storytellers you admire: their tone, their pacing, their acting out a scene, and their way of becoming the story. Eventually you will adopt some techniques from the living treasures around you, and you will let other techniques go as you form your own style.

And this is the craft of storytelling. After a while, each storyteller's technique will evolve so that your name is known far and wide, and you will have people who acknowledge you as a storyteller. This is easily the highest compliment I have ever received, and this is my wish for you!

So run on out there and spend time with your mentors. Maybe drive a bus for your Elders or community members and remember to listen. Or, if you know a storyteller who performs regularly in your community, ask if you can shuttle them around and help get the room set up for them. Ask if you can help take care of the paperwork involved and perhaps, if they are an Elder, write the thank you letters for them after a performance. Let them know that you want to become a storyteller just like them and wish to be an apprentice.

I know this can sound intimidating, but most storytellers would be honoured to know that someone wishes to learn as much as they can from you.

Don't be afraid to bring your mentor gifts: salmon, blueberries, tobacco, etc. are always a great idea. Honour your mentors and they shall mentor you.

When I travel to the North, I always stop at the homes of Elders I adore. We laugh, visit, gossip (share concerns about what's hurting our families in our community), and catch up. But after we have that out of the way, most Elders will start telling me stories about their families, their lives, the history of Fort Smith—and I listen. I listen with everything inside of me. I'm recording, in my own way, the stories Elders are gifting me with because one day someone may ask me to share a story about this Elder when they are on the other side, and I shall be able to. Even better? When an Elder asks me to record a story for their family and/or their community, this is such an honour because we will have this forever.

Another thing about visiting mentors is you can keep asking them questions about certain stories until you get the story right. I still go back and ask Elders questions to make certain I'm not messing up their stories. And I always walk away wiser, humbler, and armed with new appreciation for the living treasures of our town—our Elders.

STORYTELLING TIP #6: FIND AN APPRENTICE

As a storyteller, it is your duty to share your stories wherever you go. It is also your responsibility to find an apprentice and really train them in a good way to remember your stories. This way, you know that your stories and the stories you've been trusted with will live on in the way you want them to.

****STORYTELLING TIP #7: DRESS FOR SUCCESS

Here's something else that's very important that I want to share with you. Make sure you dress up as a story-teller. Even standup comics dress up, eh! Get spruced up for every occasion. It's important. You'll find as you are getting ready to share your stories and you're put-ting your fancy clothes on that you are in a ritual of preparing yourself to honour your audience—hey, see my author photo at the back of this book! See, I am wearing my fancy vest, and I prepared myself! Often I will pray and ask for guidance so I leave each person and place better than I found them. I will also pray that I do not offend anyone and that I leave each per-son with a lighter spirit and a full heart. That is my wish every time.

A good storyteller stands if they are able and faces the audience. I have seen time and time again that a storyteller who sits despite being able to rise out of their chair will nine times out of ten not establish the crucial link that a good visit entails. Because I am able, I always stand because this opens up your body for sound and movement. It also welcomes energy so you can move fast with the story or slow down if you need to. If you are showing how tired someone is, it is very hard to do while sitting. Also, people do not want to be craning their necks to see you.

Get that podium and mic out of the way. Those block the link between you and your audience. Trust me on this—if you don't need a mic, get it out of the way, but make sure all can hear. If you are speaking to 2,000 people, then by all means use the mic but try and make it a wireless mike or one of those doodads that goes around your ear.

Remember that it is important to stand and deliver your story in a good way if you can. Your voice and body movements and facial expressions are often your tools to becoming the story. If you cannot stand and move, remember to use your voice and all the other tips I've included below.

STORYTELLING TIP #8: HAVE FUN AND BECOME THE STORY

There are many ways to become the story—voice, facial expressions, movement, acting, even just using your fingers! Yes, put your stories into your fingers. I have had the privilege of witnessing the greatest storytellers alive, and they talk with their hands: two fingers together, trigger fingers, arms out, even using their hands to smack or tangle each other. Put your stories in your hands by using your stories to become your hands.

Raise or lower your voice. Go for it. Do impersonations. It's fun when someone raises their voice or lowers it or speaks very quickly or slowly to become the voice of the person you're honouring or humoring.

Your goal should be to have people laughing all the way home or thinking about your stories and sharing them years after you've told them. They should remember that you gave your very best, that you spoke from the heart, and that your wishes were only for the very best for everyone in the room at the time.

If you are able to move, maybe you need to move stage-left because you feel there's a bit too much chitter chatter going on over there and you want those kids to know you are aware of their energy—then head on over there. If you want to start hopping around the stage to show what it feels like to have your tail on fire as in a coyote story, by all means start hopping! The point here is that a great story can get you or your audience even moving around making a clown out of yourself or them or just energizing the space with your action and voice. The key here is for you to enjoy yourself. You're a storyteller. This gives you a passport to get on up on stage and really have fun. Do your best imitations—hang your head and limp when you speak of the wounded, dance and prance around the stage if you are talking about your crazy uncles—do whatever you have to to deliver that story in the best way.

Or sit down and tell your story only using your voice and your hands. Remember, get those fingers going. Stretch out. Claim the room.

The key here is to practice, practice, practice. Intone. Out tone. Sway each way and that when you're look-ing for something. Use that silence. Claim that silence to announce what's coming. Get in close with your audience. Walk around the room. Claim the terri-tory. Remember, a bird defines its territory by its song. Become the song.

And this is how you become the story: you embody it—if you can, act it out, but always, whether you can move around the room or not, always give one hundred percent of yourself and you will never lose. People really want to see you enjoy yourself. If they know you've given a hundred percent and have had fun yourself, they will really enjoy your time with you.

Uncle promises!

STORYTELLING TIP #9: USE THE SILENCE

Okay, so just now, above, I mentioned silence.

Silence.

Silence is like fire.

We respect and fear it. Some of us don't know what to do with it.

As a storyteller, I use it for effect and to grab one's attention. Right away. People who hear me share, know I take my time telling a story, giving it the time and dignity it deserves.

The next time you tell a story, don't cheap out. Use silence between stories or before you share a story to truly capture someone's attention.

Practice this with some more homework. When it's your time to tell a story, I want you to look down and not say anything for at least ten seconds before looking up and beginning. Feel everyone's attention summoned during that time. Use that focus on you to take your listeners where the story wishes.

STORYTELLING TIP #10: HONOUR YOUR AUDIENCE

Recently I spoke at the University of Washington by invitation of the Centre for Canadian Studies. I was asked to speak about Indigenous Literature in Canada. As I walked in, I was very surprised to see at least twenty gigantic football players in the back row. Most of them had their laptops open, and they were obviously a very close team who had their own codes of conduct.

I was not expecting this at all. But, you see, the professor was a wrestling and boxing legend on campus, and these students studied both sports with him when they weren't dominating the USA with their skill as football players.

Everything I wanted to do went out the window as soon as I saw that the majority of the students in the room were very tough men who were used to training and dishing out some punishment.

I was a bit worried about the laptops. I understand that at a university some students like to take notes during a lecture, but I could tell the students were downloading music, updating their Facebook statuses, and reading emails.

As I introduced myself, I started to make eye contact with each of the football players there, and I started to talk about how when we were growing up in the Northwest Territories my grandparents were very powerful medicine people and how people would travel for miles to see them to be prayed for. I talked about how my grandfather cured a boy who stuttered. I spoke about how my grandmother was trained as someone who brought peace to those who were getting ready to pass on. I spoke about how frustrated I was that I could not speak directly to my grandparents as they were very traditional Tłı̨chǫ Dene. Instead of learning Tłı̨chǫ, my mother's language, I had to learn French from kindergarten through grade twelve. As I spoke, I spoke softly. The students who had been whispering to each other in the beginning were now no longer talking. Many of the guys at the back started to close their laptops.

I spoke sincerely and quietly and from the heart. I spoke to them as an honoured guest with something to say, and they could all relate in their own way to what I was saying. Some of us were the same age; yet I came .from a different place with a different background. I am very fair, and they were surprised when I greeted them in Tłıchǫ. They were touched when I told them about how Irene Sanderson cured her brother's gangrene using beaver castors. I asked if anyone in the room had asthma. When the biggest guy there raised his hand (shyly), I told them that there is an Elder in our hometown, Maria Brown, who has cured many people with asthma using goose grease.

My lecture went out the window because what I felt as soon as I walked in the room was that the class wanted to learn something magical. They wanted a visit, and visiting is becoming a lost art in so many ways.

I only had fifty minutes with them, but I used it in a good way to honour them and speak to them gently and respectfully, and they were very appreciative when I was done.

What a joy that visit was!

Had I stuck to my lecture, I'm sure the laptops would have stayed up, the whispering in the back row would have continued, and we all would have lost out on something I'm sure we will all remember. I hope so anyways!

By reading your audience so you honour them—not scold them—you are getting a sense of what the audience is expecting and what they want or even need. If your talk has been set up as a lecture, this is fine. But if your audience in the lecture has been sitting through lecture after lecture and are getting a bit long in the face, why not take time for the joy and connection of storytelling instead? This is how my Ancestors have always imparted their wisdom and knowledge; besides, it's good medicine for everyone.

STORYTELLING TIP #11: CHECK OUT THE
ROOM YOU'RE SHARING STORIES IN

In the time before COVID, I was asked to close a conference at the University of Alberta. I'd never been in the room that was outlined in the contract, so I went to the first session. Thank goodness I did because it was wired for sound with huge screens present for video and video presentations. Each of the two presenters I watched had problems with the lapel microphones. I knew that at the end of the day, the participants would be tired. They'd need some get up and go stories. I also knew that I had to lose the technology as it can be very distracting. I also knew to use a hand-held microphone so I could concentrate and make eye contact with the audience.

It was a success! I asked the technician to raise all the screens and turn off the projector light. I stood and used the mic stand as my base and I didn't use any notes. I told hilarious miracle stories and quizzed them on their knowledge of the North. Oh, we had fun. The key was connecting human to human. I am finding my way in the world as someone who is starving to know not only my mother's language but all languages in the North. I'm in love with Cree, and I think I connected with the audience because we all want the same thing: to bridge where we're at with where we want to be. But had I not gone to the earlier sessions, the technology that day would have gotten in the way, and I would have been off my game.

So, I repeat, thank goodness I went to that first session.

If you are presenting professionally or even informally, learn your room. Study it. What's working for the presenters and what does the audience deserve? When you begin speaking, where will they be in their ability to concentrate and enjoy?

I knew they were all going to be tired and full, so I ended with funny stories and I stayed under my time. I stopped when I saw the first person look at their watch. It was magic.

Remember to read your audience. What do they want? What are they expecting? What's your message? How do you want to uplift them? How do you want them to remember you?

Storytelling presentations are like life—you need to be prepared. Do all you can to be ready, and try your best to be in control about how you want to be remembered long after you leave the stage.

STORYTELLING TIP #12: ASK FOR FEEDBACK

When you are finished sharing your stories, ask the audience if they have any questions. This is important. It is very easy to lose yourself in the stories that want to be told. Perhaps you've missed following up on a family you spoke about or perhaps someone in the audience is curious as to how someone you spoke about is doing today.

This is a good way to invite participation from your audience and can often lead to great discussion and, hopefully, even more storytelling.

Often when I am done sharing stories, I save ten to fifteen minutes at the end for exactly this. It is a great way to hear comments and to invite others to share their thoughts with the group. It is also a great way to close the bond you've created in a good way.

At the same time, you are inviting feedback from your audience as to how you did. I think it is always wise to remain a student of any craft. That way, if you keep hearing that people do not understand something you have said, then it is best to revisit that story and make it so that your message is clear.

Mahsi.

STORYTELLING TIP #13: GET INVOLVED WITH YOUR LOCAL STORYTELLING COMMUNITY

If you are nervous about finding a community for your storytelling, why not have a full moon ceremony in which you have a feast and put on some candles and get everyone to share a story? Remember though to be safe, following whatever safety guidelines may be in place. This is a gentle ceremony in which everyone is honoured—it's very informal and a lot of fun.

If you want, why not start up a storytelling group where you get together at a local coffee shop and share stories? Many coffee houses now have an open mike evening and would be happy for the business. Or in the age of COVID—hey! Let's Zoom!

There are usually storytelling festivals in larger cities. This is a great chance to listen to storytellers from all over the world. There are often open mike events for people to get on up there and share a story or two with an audience, even if it's online—COVID didn't stop us from sharing our stories all across the world.

The key is to get up there—or log on—and share a story. Once you've done it, you'll be so happy you did, and the feedback is immediate. If people see that you are up there in a good way wishing to share something that is magic to you, you can't lose.

The more involved you are in your storytelling community, the more it will grow—I promise. Soon there will be invitations to speak at schools, conferences, festivals, and other places.

If you keep getting your name out there as someone who is professional, does great work, has a lot of fun, and gets the audience laughing and feeling great—what's not to love? Do this and the people will be grateful because you're honouring them by sharing what you know, what you've been trusted with. You are a caretaker of stories now. You carry medicine for others and the medicine is there when you need it. ☺

STORYTELLING TIP #14: TIMING IS EVERYTHING

Be on time and don't go overtime.

STORYTELLING TIP #15—THE MOST IMPORTANT OF ALL TIPS: KEEP YOUR PROMISES

You know what you said you'd do, so do it.

A storyteller is a person of their word. Words matter. "Words become true," my son Edzazii said to me on November 15, 2020. He was six that day, and he's right.

Mahsi cho.

STORYTIME

24.
WE ARE ALL RELATED

Okay now, who wants to hear some stories! Let's do it. Here's one of my favourites.

When I was growing up in Fort Smith, I used to marvel at the artwork of Mr. George Littlechild. George is Cree. His family is from Maskwacis, Alberta. His Cree name is Nenekawasis. George's artwork graced the library walls of Paul William Kaeser High School when I was a student there serving many, many detentions (I guess you could say me, my mullet, my pinch hickeys, and my big lips used to have a BAD ATTITUDE!). I marveled at George Littlechild's ability to bring light and dignity to all of his models. Little did I know as a teenager that Mr. Littlechild would later illustrate two of my children's books: *A Man Called Raven* and *What's the Most Beautiful Thing You Know About Horses?* Can you imagine my surprise at not only being able to work with one of my greatest heroes but to meet him, tour with him across Canada and the United States, and now be able to call him one

George and I were given during our last tour together across northern BC. George and I had the privilege of working with community members and kindergarten to grade twelve students, courtesy of our host, the late Leo Sabulsky. Leo was the fire chief and owner of several businesses in Chetwynd, BC, which has 3,000 people. Leo was also a huge advocate for family literacy, and he secured some funds to bring George and me up for a series of workshops, readings, and community story-telling events. It was so much fun. Leo was hilarious and such a generous host.

***

One night, after a day of working in the schools, Leo shared a story with us that I have his permission to share with you now. He said a long time ago, before Chetwynd grew to the grand size it is today, there was an Elder there named Grandma Mavis. Grandma Mavis ran Chetwynd. Sure, there was a mayor, chief, and band council, but Grandma Mavis understood the importance of family and community. Because Leo was the fire chief back then, and because Grandma Mavis was the unofficial boss of Chetwynd, Leo often ended up at her house after a house fire so he could consult with her on what to do next for the displaced family or families. Grandma Mavis knew how to motivate community members and local businesses to make sure that if the family was involved in a house fire, they would be taken care of properly.

One night after a particularly horrendous fire, Leo was exhausted. He nodded off at her supper table and woke to find her watching him.

"Oh, Granny," Leo said. "I'm sorry I fell asleep. Why don't we keep talking about this tomorrow morning?"

"Leo," Granny Mavis asked," how are we related?"

"Granny," Leo said, "I am pretty sure we are not related. You are Cree and Beaver. You are a Creever. I am Ukrainian. I am very sure we are not related."

"Leo, Leo, Leo," Granny Mavis said. "We are all family—and I can prove it to you. Give me a couple days and I'll figure out how we are related."

Well, you know, folks, it only took her a good night's sleep before she called him again. "Leo? It's Granny Mavis," she said. "I figured out how we are related."

"Granny?" Leo asked. "How?"

"Your dog is the son of my dog," she said.

***

And it was true—Leo's dog was the son of her dog and they were family, after all. He said to us, "You know how many times I used that little nugget of gold to open doors over the years?"

My friends, we are all family. Whether it's through our dogs, cats, faith, goldfish, music, laughter, stories, dancing, life—we are all family. I'm not kidding. This is serious business for my community: the term *all my relations* is true and so important. Even Western scientists prove every day the teachings that my Ancestors have always known. And these stories of being all family, all related, even the non-humans, *everything*, these stories can do more to unite us and bring peace than most anything else I believe. Rest in Power, Leo. Mahsi cho for all your service, leadership, and friendship.

25.
SPIRIT STORIES

Get ready for a spirit story you'll never forget. In the early 1990s, I interviewed Anna Tonasket, a Syilx (Okanagan) Nation storyteller. Incredible, hey, that nearly thirty years later, with her permission, I can now share this story with you? That's why I want you to head out and start recording (if they're okay with it) your cousins and uncles and Elders and friends. Here's the story that Anna told me one day that, again, changed my life forever.

***

So you want to know about the Little People? I was born and raised in Vernon, BC. We're about twenty miles out of the city of Vernon. That's where I was raised. We had a home that's situated on about thirty-three acres, and half of the land is cleared. The other half still has the trees and the siya bushes and whatnot. Anyways, there's this creek that runs through our property on an angle. From our new house it's just about—oh, I'd say 500 feet from where our old house was. When we were young, my mom and dad would go to town, to Vernon, and they would leave us by ourselves from the time we were seven or eight because we had what my mother called babysitters. These babysitters were what she called "the Little People." As I was growing up, we called them "Jokers."

So my friends would come over. They had no problem coming over during the day—or any of my other relatives—but they would not come once it got dark because they said they could hear people in what we called our forest. I was never afraid of the dark. For some reason I felt at ease once it was dark, especially on our own land, on our own property. My sister, my brother, and I, we used to go and play in the woods. Mom's rule was, "You be home by dark." But as long as we were within our thirty-three acres, we were home. So we would go out and we would play.

And this one part in the creek when you got close to it you could hear voices. You could hear people laughing. I've never seen one of the Little People. I've only heard them. But my Uncle Angus—he was quite old and he still lived in the old shack across the road from our place—and he used to come up because we had TV when we moved into our new house when I was six years old. We had electricity, so we got a TV. My mom and dad had bought us a black and white TV. So my uncle used to come up in the evenings and he'd watch TV. At eleven o'clock he would say, "Well, I'm going to go home." And he'd bid us all good night. My uncle only spoke Syilx (Okanagan). He never spoke a word of English throughout the whole time I knew him. All he spoke was our language. So he'd tell us good night and, by this time, us kids were supposed to be in bed. Being kids, we'd goof around and stay up and we'd still be awake, and we'd hear Uncle leave.

Well, there was this big puddle about halfway down our road. The dirt road was about a quarter a mile long from the highway to our house. About half of the way there was this big dip in the road, and when it rained or after the snow melted, there'd be this huge puddle. And we had what we called shoppy trees, and we used them like California people would use palm trees— we'd sit under them and we'd play. But, anyway, there was this apple tree and these shoppy trees lined up by this puddle. My uncle could not pass that big puddle. Something would not let him go. And he says it was the Little People. They wouldn't allow him to cross, and it was about a hundred feet before the creek crossed the road. But they wouldn't let him pass this big puddle and he would try. He tried so many times to get home. He wanted to go home but something just wouldn't let him. He'd get this chill down his back spine. Like the hair on the back of his neck would literally stand up. He would try and take a step and he just couldn't. He'd end up turning around and coming [back], spending the night. But if he was bound and determined to go home, one of us kids would have to get up, which was usually me as I was the oldest. I would walk my uncle home, and nothing would bother us. He would be talking to me in Syilx (Okanagan) saying, "I couldn't get past this spot, you know. How come you can bring me home?"

And I'd tell him, "I don't know, Uncle."

So we'd go, and I'd take him home and then I would come back and I'd go to bed. This went on until my uncle died. It got to a point where he would leave before dusk because any time after dusk he just couldn't. The only way he could get home is if my dad drove him home, and he never liked to ask my dad to drive him because it was within walking distance. So I would get up and I would take him home.

When our house was being renovated, we lived with my uncle and my qa'qna, which is my dad's mother, and my grand-aunt, my gramma's sister, Aunty Elizabeth. Uncle Angus used to always tell us, being kids and being curious we'd hear things outside and right now we'd [look out the window] to see what's out there, who's out there, and he would come and he'd be yakking at us in Syilx (Okanagan), telling us: "Don't look out the window. Something will look back at you. Humas are out there."

Humas means "Bogey Man." Bogey man's out there. We thought they were just trying to scare us.

But anyway, my uncle would see these Little People and they would tease him when he would go to the outhouse—they'd knock on the side of the outhouse. He thought it was us at first. He'd be hollering at us kids, "Leave me alone! I'm in the outhouse!"

And he'd come back in and he would tell Mom, "Shouldn't be letting those kids outside. It's dark."

And my mom would tell him in Syilx (Okanagan), "They're sleeping."

And Uncle would come, and he would check. At first it would baffle him, and he got kind of leery. And so he said, one time, he said he was sitting in the outhouse and he whips open the door, and he was convinced it was one of us kids playing tricks. He whips open the door and he seen this little person. All he could tell us was this little person had big, black, coal eyes. They were just black. But the body was kind of transparent. But he said it looked like a little human, other than the skin wasn't brown, it wasn't white. It was just sort of transparent. And he said he could see them running and playing like little kids having fun, always laughing.

One time my cousin Debbie had come to visit me. I told her, "Well, I'll walk you home."

Her mom phoned and said it was time for her to come on home. So I said, "Okay, I'll walk you home." But I told her, "But I want to cut through the forest."

And Debbie was scared to death of what we called our forest!

She said, "No. I don't want to go through there!"

"But it's the shortcut! This is how we'll get you home faster!"

She said, "There's something in your woods!"

I said, "There is nothing in there. We play in there! It's like playing in our house." She said, "No, no."

I told her, "Well, if you want me to walk you home, we have to go through that way because I don't feel safe walking by the highway because you never know!" We lived like how many miles from town, right? We're way out in the boonies—or so we thought at the time. So I convinced her we were going through the woods because it was the short way. Anyway, we got about halfway through, and all of a sudden she grabs me, and she's two years older than I am, and she whips me in front of her and she says, "Anna, Anna! There's something over there!"

And I'm looking through the dark and I'm listening, and I said, "Aww, must be the neighbour's cow!"

She says, "No, no, Anna. Someone's running!"

You could see them dashing. They're hiding from us! "Aww, it's probably just the Little People."

Well, of course, she just freaked right out. She wanted to turn around right there and then. She wanted my dad to drive her home. I said, "No, we're already halfway there. We only had five minutes to walk and we're off of our property. We could cut through Robert's field, and the ball diamond, get on the road, and you're home, right?"

But Debbie was just petrified. She kept saying, "There's somebody out there. Can't you see them?"

Being accustomed to being on my own property and knowing that there were these Little People, I was never scared of them. I've never come face to face with one, mind you. You could hear them laugh, like kids playing. It sounds like kids playing. And it never bothered me. My thought as a youngster was, well, if I can't see them, right? Because it's dark, they can't see me, either. It was comforting to me when it was nighttime because that was my way of thinking: if I can't see them, they can't see me.

Mom always used to tell us, "I never have to worry about you kids. That's why I can leave you when Dad and I go to town, we go out"—or whatever they're going to do in town—"and I know you kids are going to be fine."

And they left us a lot and there was just myself and my younger brother and my sister. There was just the three of us except the odd time when some of our cousins would come and stay. But, other than that, mostly it was three of us.

Once Mom and Dad were out of sight, we'd build a fort, we'd wreck it, and we'd start all over again, and we could hear [the Little People]. With us it wasn't actually seeing them. It was like a shadow. Like catching something in the corner of your eye and you look but there's nothing there. As we got closer to where the creek is on our property you could hear them laughing. I can't recall hearing words or hearing them talking. All I remember is laughing. They seemed like they were happy Little People. And other than my Uncle Angus, I've never known them to bother anybody; but for some reason, like I said, my uncle, he could not go home by himself. A lot of times he would spend a lot of nights on our couch because we'd be sleeping, and he wouldn't want to bother my dad cuz my dad works at four o' clock in the morning and he's up at three and he has to travel a distance to go to work. So my uncle didn't want to bother him, so he would end up staying and, as soon as it got daylight, well, he'd go home knowing it was safe. He could head home.

Anyway, Debbie, she flat out refused to come to my place. If it was after dark and we had to be together, we had to be at her place because she would not go through the woods after that one time. She swore that there was something or someone out there and they were watching us. She could see them, but not really.

And as I was growing up, I thought she was such a big chicken. She was two years older and she was putting me in front of her. Give me a break!

That's what I know about the Little People. They never bothered us. And if anything, I guess what they've done is they've protected us while we were by ourselves because nothing, no one, would come around the house. No one would come.

There was this one time, my dad would go to the Vernon Vikings hockey games and I wasn't much of a hockey fan. I liked to watch my dad and I liked to watch my uncles, my family play. This was a non-Native team and I never did care, you know, for sports on TV or to watch someone I don't know play. It never did interest me. It had to be someone I knew before I would sit and watch . . . So they wanted to go to a hockey game, and my brother and sister wanted to go because they had a concession, which meant french fries. So that's the only reason they went.

I never did go to town, even as a teenager, basically to school and back. Anyway, they left and they said, "We'll be home 11:30/12 o'clock." I said, "Yeah, okay."

My mom, that one night . . . usually when they leave it's, "Bye, Anna, see you later. I love you. Lock the doors, blah blah blah, and keep the lights on."

My mom always used to tell me, "Keep the lights on."

But I never liked the lights on. I couldn't sleep if there was a light on. My sister and I are like day and night. She couldn't sleep without the lights on. And I would wait for her to go to sleep and I would turn the hall light off and the bathroom light off. And as soon as I would turn everything off, she'd wake up!

So anyway, this one night I was left by myself. Mom and Dad went, and Vina and Pierre went to the hockey game. I used to just sit in the dark and listen to my radio or my record player. And I was sitting in the living room one night. That night, it was a Sunday night, and I must have been about thirteen years old.

It didn't dawn on me that my mother had been over concerned because that wasn't the first time I was left totally by myself. But for some reason she kept saying, "Make sure you lock the doors." She showed me where my dad's gun was. My dad showed me where the gun's bullets were. And this is something they had never done. Mom was really apprehensive about leaving me, and I kept telling her, "What's your problem? It's not like this is the first time. I mean, how many times have I willingly chose to be by myself?"

That's just how I was. I needed my own time.

Anyway, she gave me all these instructions.

They were gone for a half hour, forty-five minutes, hour maybe, and all of a sudden, I seen these lights come up. And like I said, our house was a quarter mile from the highway. So you could see the headlights the minute the car turned itself on the property. And I thought someone took the wrong road because the next-door neighbours . . . they had visitors all the time on either side of our property. One was an elderly man with three daughters, and they had visitors coming all the time. And on the other side of us was the Louis family, and they were cattle people, rodeo people, so they had cowboys and cattle men coming over to their place and they would be given directions, and they would end up coming up to our place and we would just redirect them. But, anyway, I seen this car coming up. I thought, "Aw, somebody got lost again."

But as they got closer, I got more and more nervous. I had all the lights off, so to them, maybe nobody was home. What I thought was, "They would see no lights. They would turn around and they would leave."

Well, they parked on the side of the house. And I was scared to look out of the curtains because I thought, "Well, geez, I can see pretty good out there. They may be able to see in just as good, right? If they see this curtain move, they're gonna know somebody's home." So I was trying to look through the slit of the curtain, I was trying to see. There was this dark vehicle parked there and three of what I thought were young men got out. They tried the back door. Locked. Someone came around the front, checked the front door. They started checking the living room windows. We had sticks to block the windows because we had gotten our house broken into a few times, and the windows were just really crappy. They couldn't lock very well. So my dad had cut these sticks to match all the windows and they couldn't budge any of the windows. And you could hear them talking. And they were saying, "Well, they leave their kids by themselves. They have a daughter. She's a teenager."

My heart was just a pounding. I went into the living room closet where my dad's gun was, and I went into the kitchen where the bullets were in the kitchen, in one of the drawers. And I was trying to be quiet. And you know how when you're trying to be quiet, the house naturally creaks and stuff, eh? And I thought, "Oh my god. They're going to hear me. They're going to break the door down."

I opened the butcher knife drawer. I got out three of the biggest butcher knives we had, stuck them between the doors and the panel, the side panelling there, and the door, although the door was locked, and hearing this guy say, "Well, they have a teenage daughter. They leave their kids alone," and they were laughing, and you could hear bottles clinking. There were actually bottles where this car was parked when my dad got home. Anyway, I got scared. So I went and put the butcher knives in the door. I already had the gun. So I went, I got the drawer open. But being dark, I didn't know if I had the right bullets. I had the .22 gun. There were .22 bullets. There was a .303, a .30-30. There was shotgun bullets. And being scared, I was trying to be quiet and I thought, well if I start making noise they're going to hear. And you could hear them talking. And all of a sudden you could hear, "What's that? Did you see that!? What's that!" Then all of a sudden, "Let's get the hell out of here!"

They jumped in their car, they spun around in our yard. And they took off down the road, and you could hear this faint, this faint little laugh.

And my parents got home about midnight, and I was still up. I had to undo the butcher knives because they couldn't get in the house with the keys and Mom was yelling, "Anna, it's Mom! Open the door! Anna, Anna Jean! Are you awake?"

And my dad's banging on the door. And I'm, "Is that really you, Mom? Is that really you?"

And I was scared to turn the porch light on.

Mom: "Turn the light on. You'll see it's me and Dad!"

So I flipped the porch light on and looked out the dining room window and, sure enough, it's my parent's car out there, so I take the three butcher knives out and my dad walks in: "What the hell's wrong with you? Why do you have these butcher knives stuck in the door for?"

And my mom took one look at me, and I must have been just pale because I was really scared. I kept thinking, "They're going to come back. They're going to come back."

And my mom said, "What's the matter? What's wrong? Are you sick? You are so pale."

I'm fair to begin with.

Dad said, "Who the hell was here?"

My dad just knew. I don't know, maybe it was the tire tracks. My dad knew every time someone came to our house. He just knew. He said he could tell by the road. I figure it was the tire tracks.

But he says, "Who the hell was here?"

I told him, "I don't know."

And he says, "What did I tell you about inviting people over when we're not home?"

And I said, "Dad, I didn't invite anybody over."

And then I started telling him how this car came up, how these guys were checking the doors, the windows, how I overheard them saying that we get left alone, and that they have a teenage daughter, and I said, "And the funny thing is all of a sudden it was like somebody scared them off."

My mom says, "I knew it."

I'm looking at her going, "You knew what?"

She says, "I told you. I never have to worry about you kids when I leave you home alone. You have babysitters. You have people who look out for you."

She's talking, like in circles to me, and she says, "I bet you anything it was the Little People that scared these boys away."

I told my mom what they had said: "What's that? What's that? Let's get the hell out of here."

Something had frightened them.

That was the one time, in all my years—I lived in Vernon for fifteen years 'til I was fifteen, and then I moved away on my own. That was the only time I have ever gotten scared. I was scared. I was panic stricken. And I still, to this day, believe it was the Little People that helped me. Mom said they were always there. She never, ever worried about us. As long as she knew we were within our property, we were okay. Nothing or no one would bother us . . .

* * *

Anna is from the Syilx (Okanagan) Nation. She told this to me in her home on the Penticton Indian Reserve in the summer of 1995. She is the mother of Cash, Elliott, Destiny, and Harmony. She was born September 19, 1961. I recorded this in 1992 and transcribed it word for word with Anna's permission. I was able to email this recording as an MP3 file twenty-two years later, and now it is available on my SoundCloud account (find the link in the Resources on page 189). It transformed me because it affirms that the ancient magic of the world is still here, still protecting special people.

Now here's more homework: go interview someone your own age who has a story that just blows you away that you want the whole world—and all generations to come—tto know about. With their permission, and following proper protocol, transcribe it for them word for word, gift it back to them, and make sure they are happy with what you've done. Ask if they are happy with what they read, and if they want to make changes, make those changes with them. Print it up and go through it again. Take their portrait. They now have a gift for their family and friends: a recording of their story, the story written out, and their portrait. This is how I've collected so many stories all these blessed years. Their family will always thank you, and so will their friends. I think this is a lovely way to be in the world: one who honours, one who cherishes, one who helps people remember.

26.
A TRANSFORMATIVE STORY

There's a Lakota saying: "May the Great Mystery always put a sunrise in your heart."

Get ready for a story that will swoon your soul.

I was told this story a few decades ago by Pauline Clarke. As she shared it, I was wishing I had my tape recorder. Thanks to email, I begged Pauline to rewrite it so I could share it. She did something even better. She got her brother to write his part too.

Here's the story of a lifetime. Mahsi cho to Pauline and Barrie for agreeing to share their incredible story of fate that, I hope, will renew your belief in the circle of life.

***

GATHER

PAULINE CLARKE

On the shorelines of Davin Lake, Saskatchewan, stands a lonely but not forgotten cross, a cross that was laid there in memory of a loved one who passed on.

It was in the early eighties. My family lived on a trap line in northeastern Saskatchewan. We would live there throughout the summer and move back into the community when school season started. Life on the trap line was simple but you had to be tough to survive. There were six children in my family, myself being the youngest. My mother and father were hard working people, and they did the best they could to raise us with whatever they had. They always taught us to be proud of what we had, never envy others, and always be respectful. Now life was not always simple. When we had to move back to the community we were faced with social problems like alcoholism and domestic abuse.

My brother Barry and I were the closest to each other because we were the youngest in our family. He was three years older than I was. We basically grew up hand in hand. When times were tough we always stuck by each other. I always knew that I could count on my brother whenever I needed him. I rarely ever turned to my older siblings; they were in their own worlds. I trusted Barry more because I knew he would protect me from being hurt or scared. A vivid memory that always comes back to me is a time when we were afraid. I was even more afraid because there was a fight breaking out at home, and I hid underneath the bed. My brother came to me and he said, "Don't be scared, Sister. I will always be here to take care of you." Of course, he said this in Cree: "Kawitha sikisi nisimis kapi kikakitapamitin."

We went about our adolescence, going to school in the community and then returning to the trap line in the summer months. Barry had to move away from the community in order to attend high school in La Ronge because in those days the grades only went up to grade nine. So Barry moved into town. By this time my parents were sober and had been for a couple of years. It was in late October when he phoned home to tell the parents that he wanted to come home because he was lonely. He wanted to go back to the trap line. So in the beginning of November he came back home, and my father prepared for their trip to the trap line. A couple days before they left, Barry did a lot of visiting. He made sure that he visited every one of his friends. Before he walked out of the door, he made sure he said farewell to all of us and he left.

A few days later he got into an accident that took his young life.

My father says that they were out hauling logs for their camp in the shores of Davin Lake. They stopped by the end of the lake on the last bay. Barry was carrying a loaded gun on one side and a log on the other. The shores on the lake had ice along the shores and it was slippery. Barry tripped and fell, shooting himself right through the heart. My dad had to carry him to the boat and drove him to the other side where the road was. When he got to land, he had to carry him over his shoulders and walked three kilometres to the main road. He said he tripped over so many times but the only thing he could think about was saving his son and getting him to safety.

The first vehicle that came up to my father was Sask-Tel, so they phoned for a chopper to come down, but it was too late. When my brother took his last breath, my father said he smiled and pointed up towards Heaven.

The devastation I felt when I heard my brother was hurt was overwhelming. I had not yet heard that he actually died. I thought he was just injured, and I couldn't bear the thought of him having serious injuries. I cried, I felt so sorry for him. When I got home, I was even more surprised to find the police, priest, and close family friends surrounding my mother. My father hadn't arrived from the accident yet. I went to my mother and she hugged me and told me that my brother was gone and that he was not going to be coming back. I broke down in tears. I could not believe he was dead, gone. I remembered Barry saying he would always be there and that he would protect me, and, as a child, I really did believe it, and I depended on him. I could not believe he was gone. He had broken his promise and I felt resentful. I was a hurting child. It took me days to come back down to reality. What upset me the most out of the whole thing was that when my dad first walked in the house all by himself, I waited for Barry to follow after him, but he did not. My father walked in alone that day. He walked straight into the room and cried like a baby. I had never heard my father cry before. It was so painful to see such a strong man cry. That was my first experience with death, and I did not like it. It was like hell.

After the accident, my father made a trip up to the lake to post up a memorial cross where the accident happened. I, of course, did not go. I was still too weak to go. I knew that if I went then that I would not be able to control myself. I felt I was not strong enough at the time.

The community felt the pain. Losing a young boy who was friends with everyone, it just made the community sad. I became a really angry teenager. I did not care about myself or anyone else. I just wanted to stay mad at God. I blamed God for taking my brother away. I didn't pray when I was forced to go to church. All I thought about was awful things about God. I was the prime enemy. I had no respect for my body. I did solvent abuse with my friends. We would start in the day and end it at night; sometimes it lasted for twelve straight hours.

When I did this, I was able to see my brother. When you inhale solvents, your mind starts to hallucinate, and you usually see something that you are thinking about. So I did this for a while. I was able to see and talk to my brother. Once I was introduced to alcohol, I quit inhalants and started a new addiction. I always had to have something to keep me out of the reality I was living in. I couldn't let my brother go. I had so much pain inside I was afraid to come out with it.

***

BARRIE CLARKE

My name is Barrie Clarke. I am a professor of geology at Dalhousie University in Halifax, Nova Scotia. Most people, including my students, don't spell my name correctly. Even my good friends write "Barry Clarke" or "Barry Clark." I'm quite used to seeing different spellings.

In the summer of 1994, I was doing geological mapping in the Davin Lake area. My normal way of operating was to cruise the shoreline in a boat, stopping to examine outcrops of rock. One day in July, my assistant Andy Henry and I entered an otherwise ordinary bay of

Davin Lake and saw a large white cross on the distant shore. Immediately I forgot all about the geology of the shoreline. In all my thirty years of doing field geology, I had never seen a cross in the woods before. I was drawn to it like a magnet, and I soon found out why. Andy was in the back of the sixteen-foot aluminium boat. I was in the front. Andy put the bow of the boat into the shore right in front of the cross. Andy could see the writing on the cross but was not able to read it. I was just staring and speechless, so Andy asked, "What does it say?" I replied, "Andy, it has my name on it!" (The spelling of my name wasn't quite right, but, of course, I'm used to that.)

Now it would be a very strange coincidence for anyone to find a cross in the remote woods with their name on it, but in my case, this was even stranger. The last movie I had watched on TV before coming to Saskatchewan was about a brother and a sister. The brother had been killed in an accident but had returned to the land of the living as a spirit without knowing that he had died. He did what he came back to do, and then at the end of the movie, his sister took him to his grave and showed him his name on the headstone. Then he realized that he had died in the accident. For a few moments there at Barry's cross, I was very bewildered. I wondered if the same thing was happening to me. Had I died doing field work at Davin Lake? Was Andy taking me to my memorial? It was the most peculiar feeling I have ever had. I didn't know what was true anymore. Was I dreaming? I briefly lost my connection with reality.

When my reason took control of my emotion, I began to develop a very strong sense of empathy toward my young namesake. I very much needed to find out who Barry Clarke was and what tragic event had happened at this place. I wanted to find out who had so lovingly erected this cross. Had anyone ever found the cross except me? It almost seemed as if the cross was put there so I would find it. These questions had to wait several agonizing weeks until we were finished our work. Eventually I left the field and returned to places where I could search for answers to some of my questions, but all I was able to learn was that Barry had been a resident of Southend. So when I returned to Halifax, I wrote a letter (next page), bought a bouquet of dried flowers, and sent them simply addressed to "The Clarke Family Who Lost a Son at Davin Lake in 1987, Southend, Saskatchewan, S0J 2L0" and hoped that the package would reach the right people.

* * *

PAULINE CLARKE

It was in 1994 when I went for a mail run at our local Hudson Bay store. Our post office has general delivery so there are no separate mailboxes. I was in the line-up when the employee invited me to the back. She showed me this parcel which wrote, "To the Clarke Family who lost their loved one in Davin Lake in 1987." It had B. Clarke, Halifax Nova Scotia, as the return address. The employee knew that it belonged to my family, so she gave it to me. For a while, I thought, "Oh my God. I think my brother is alive." Then I realized that I really did see him in his casket and, yes, I did see him getting buried six feet underground, so I knew it wasn't him, even though the handwriting looked like his. So I went home with the parcel.

When I got home, my parents were in the living room watching television. My mom knew that there was something going on when I walked in. She asked me what was going on, so I told them to sit down because I had some news. So I sat them down and told them about our package. I opened it, and there was a bouquet of dried-up roses, a letter, and a sympathy card. I started reading the letter but could not finish it right away. The letter came from this man named Barrie Clarke from Halifax, Nova Scotia, a geologist who works at Dalhousie University. He wrote that he was mapping the Davin lake area in 1994 when he came upon my brother's memorial cross. This is what the letter said:

August 15, 1994
Dear Clarke Family,

Please forgive me for writing, and probably reminding you of a very sad time in the past. This summer, while I was mapping in the Davin Lake area, I found the cross that you had erected in memory of your son Barry. At first I was very startled to see 'my' name on the cross, but ever since then I have felt deep sorrow for my namesake, and for you too. The cross was a very strong indication to me of how much you loved him, and how much you must miss him. I mourn for young Barry who was not able to live his life to the fullest. Also, as a parent myself, and with one son just a year older than Barry would be now, and I can imagine the pain that all of you experienced in losing him.

I hope you will accept the enclosed flowers in memory of young Barry. Please lay them at his resting place for me, or keep them yourselves, whatever you wish. I also sincerely hope you have now all found peace.

Yours respectfully,
Barrie Clarke

He was so stunned to see his same name on this cross, in the middle of nowhere, he immediately felt a deep connection to our family. I wasn't able to complete the reading. I fell down and I cried. I felt a cold rush of air flowing through me. It was something new, something I never felt before. I felt the inner peace that I had longed to feel for many years. I had finally been set free. I knew even before I finished reading the letter that it really came from my brother. I remembered how he told me he would always be there for me. I knew right then and there that he was always there. He never left me or my family. He made sure I was okay before he left; he left me with sober parents and an adopted sister the same age as he was. I wasn't aware of it until the parcel came to us. He was always there. He never broke his promise. For years I felt angry for nothing. It was time to let him go in peace. It took me awhile to come out with the pain I had been carrying for years, but I did it and it felt great. I never felt so free in my life. It was time to start living again.

I went to school and I made sure that I would graduate and do the things my brother Barry never had a chance to do. I always knew he was right into the music, so I started singing. I wanted my brother's spirit to live within me. I completed my grade twelve and went on to university. I took up several jobs throughout the years.

I'm still in university striving for a degree in Political Science with a certificate in Indian Communication Arts, and I will be done soon.

Ever since Barrie sent us the package in 1994, we have been in close contact with each other. My family accepted this man into the family. We usually communicate through snail mail and now email. We recently met in Regina. We met at Red Lobster, got there at the same time. It was a wonderful meeting: we talked a lot about Barry and how he lived, what he liked to do, and about our most amazing experience. I truly believe in fate and the power of the great beyond. I believe in a love so strong it can break all negative forces.

I told Barrie about my trip to the accident for the first time all these years. It was last month. I had never been there before, and I finally went. It was still sad for me, especially when I had to listen to my dad describe how the accident happened and what they went through. I prayed all through the time we were there. I could sense my brother's spirit there. That is where my brother loved to be, the trap line, and that is where he died. The trap line was where we felt peace. As we were leaving the site, an eagle followed us. I was even more amazed when I went to the site. How could someone from so far away come over here and find this cross? It was almost as if it was meant for Barrie to see, so that years later we would connect and form a lasting friendship in memory of my brother Barry.

Thank you. Mahsi cho.

***

BARRIE CLARKE

As you can see, my package did arrive and it resulted in the development of a warm bond between the two Clarke families, even though they were very far apart. Then, one day in the summer of 2002, I finally met the entire Southend Clarke family at Davin Lake. As we sat around the campfire talking that evening, I felt as comfortable as if I had known them for my whole life. There is much more to this connection than just a chance discovery of a white cross in the woods.

Thank you.

27.
A MIRACLE WAR STORY

n 1992, I was attending the En'owkin International School of Writing in Penticton, BC. Our Elder-in-Residence was Glen Douglas, an Syilx (Okanagan) man. Holy moley, what a man. I was working on a manuscript called *Tracking Heaven* and was writing down stories that were shared with me by my Elders in Fort Smith as I drove the Handi-Bus.

I made Glen a copy of the stories I had so far and asked him if I could tape him telling a miracle story. He agreed. I had no idea he was going to share this story about being hit by a grenade while serving in the Korean War. This was told to me on Friday, November 6 in 1992 in Penticton, BC. Glen was sixty-five then.

Get ready for soul thunder.

***

On the 17th of July, 1953, I was sent out on a patrol. There were three of us. We watched a fire fight all night long on an outpost out to our immediate front a mile away, and we were to intercept straggling enemy that were leading toward our direction, the mainline of resistance . . . we were going to intercept them and try to capture them. This was ten days before the Armistice . . . we met them right in front of our positions, about 300 yards in front of our resistance. There was a fire fight.

I remember a hand grenade being thrown, and I seen a hand grenade land by my feet. It was a concussion grenade, fortunately. Blew me off my feet. My feet went up in the air. Blew me quite high and then over . . . where we were fighting the rice had grown wild over the past three years, hadn't been harvested. It grew about eight feet and I landed in that thick rice. My other troop members didn't see me. They ran off the enemy. There were ten of them. I suppose the only thing they had was probably a few rounds of ammo and one hand grenade. I was hit across both legs. I laid there for two days before they found me. And when they did find me, they were going to put me in a rubber bag and take me and bury me, but I opened my eyes.

But as I lay there, I remember coming to. I tried to move, and I was paralyzed from the waist down. But as I felt down there, I felt blood . . . I could see I was pretty bloody down there below my waist . . . I took my belt off, my cartridge belt, and I took my bayonet and unhooked it and used my bayonet, my bayonet scabbard, to make a tourniquet, and as I tied the tourniquet, I passed out, lost consciousness . . .

It was like a dream and what it was, I was placed . . . I was told to sit down in a chair, and I sat in that chair and it started moving, and we moved into a tunnel. And as we moved into this tunnel this chair started picking up speed, but I could see on the sides of this tunnel there appeared to be lights quite a ways apart, probably a mile or so apart, but as this thing started moving so fast that the lights were just like one string, one line. That's how fast it moved, and all of a sudden it came to a stop. When this thing came to a stop, this chair I'm sitting on was [on] flat ground with a slight incline to my front. And a long ways off was a gate, and I heard a voice. It was a beautiful voice, a baritone voice, and it said, "You are welcome to join us. Follow the path to the gate and join us."

And I stood up from this chair-like vehicle and I started walking. As I walked, I noticed the grass and the flowers. The flowers I never seen in my life. I started walking, and I walked, and I walked, and I could see a well-defined path. It looked like it was manicured. The grass looked like it was cut by hand, every bit of it with flowers on either side of it. And I kept walking and walking, and pretty soon I looked down and I was wearing my dress uniform, but I had no shoes or boots. And, yet I couldn't feel the grass under my feet; but I continued walking. But it seemed I wasn't getting any closer to that gate. But on that gate there was flowers. You could read the word "Welcome," and I walked and I walked and I heard the voice again.

It said, "You, too, are welcome to join us. Follow that path."

And I knew that person was behind me. I tried to turn around and I couldn't. I tried four times. I twisted with all my might and when I did, instead of seeing anything behind me, I came through that same tunnel back to the other side. But this time, on the way, I seen a bunch of floating bodies—some of them were clothed, some of them were naked, some of them were in caskets, some of them were half clothed, just the tops with the bottoms off, just a shirt on, and they were like in water, just floating. And they took me through this area, and it was like we were underwater, and you could see these bodies floating around, going no place, just hanging in suspension. And I asked what this was all about, and they said, "These are the people who take their own lives. These are the people who take their own lives."

Then we went on, and I came to and I opened my eyes, and I was looking straight into the face of the helicopter pilot. And as I opened my eyes, I could see the change of his expression. At the same time, I seen him move his arm. He had his hand on the controls. I seen him move to the right and another face came right in front of him and he had his hand like that, with his thumb up, telling me to hang in there. And I guess they got fired on. I remember hearing shots, and they took off. They were going to put me in a rubber bag, I understand, take me and bury me, but I opened my eyes.

Well, I was conscious for a few seconds. When I opened my eyes, I could see the blue sky with tufts of clouds and I said, "Gee, I must be in Heaven." I'd already been there and didn't realize it. This is what Heaven looks like, and I passed out again.

The next time I woke up, I seen a bunch of masked faces with the lights up above us, round lights. I passed out again.

I woke up looking into the Rocky Mountains of Denver, Colorado. I was facing the windows with the hospital facing the mountains, and I woke up. And after I woke up, a few seconds later, the doctor and the nurse came by and said, "Oh, you're awake now."

I said, "Yeah, and I'm hungry and I'm thirsty!"

He said, "You're a very lucky man; you're a walking miracle."

I asked him, "What do you mean?"

He said, "Most people have twelve pints of blood, average person, twelve pints of blood, and we had to put in eleven pints into you. Most people die when they put in five pints of blood. But you, we put eleven pints of blood into you. We had a hard time to find your veins, to expand them, to put the tubes in. You're a very lucky man."

Well, that was just the beginning. I suffered four years, four months, and twenty-six days while I was in the hospital.

I was hit on the 17th of July 1953, and I left the hospital in December 1957 . . . I had a lot of pain, eighteen operations on my legs. When I left in 1957, they told me I'd never walk again—I left in a wheelchair. I managed to stay on active duty . . . I stayed in twenty-two and one-half years. After that injury, that last wound, that was my eighth time I was wounded in Korea. I went to fight another war. I went to fight in Vietnam.

And I began to question why I survived. I never knew. It didn't register with me for a while, but then I began to question: Why did I survive when so many have died?

Then I began to think about all my other experiences before then, about the things that had happened to me that would be called unusual by many people. Then I began to realize there was such a thing as Divine Intervention. The Creator was protecting me. But then I recalled other things happening; that when I was eight years old my father had sent me into the sweat lodge to sleep there because I had disobeyed him. I had lied to him. It was not the first time I had done this. In our ways, they send us there to get our vision.

I guess you would call it a vision, but what I had an experience with was a song that came. It told me, "I will be with you the rest of your life."

That's all it said to me: "Don't be afraid. I'll be with you and you'll be with me and you will not understand me until the sun starts falling," and I did not understand that which was one o'clock. I didn't understand.

I went on with my military career all through my life. This happened when I was about eight years old. And through my wartime experiences, especially when I was in Korea, I've had many incidents in there that I could have been killed. Yet I survived, and I didn't know what it was that kept me alive. I didn't know until 1986 when I had a dream. It told me several things, but four times this song, it came into my life.

The second time I heard it was when I was seventeen, going on eighteen. It was before I went overseas to the Second World War in Europe. I got sick, had pneumonia, and they had no penicillin. All their penicillin was on the battlefield. But they give me some sulpha. I stayed in the hospital thirty days. During my crisis in that bout with pneumonia, I seen my entire life in front of me. It was shown. And one of the things that was happening to me was I was in a swing, and I was getting higher and higher and it dared me to jump. I didn't know it then, but I know it now that if I had jumped, then I would have died. I wouldn't have gone on any farther; I would have been called into the spirit world. But I didn't jump. I didn't let go. I trusted; I had faith in the Creator, but I never realized it at the time, and I went on. I went on into Europe, the European battlefields. Came back safely, didn't have any close calls to speak of, but in Korea I had many.

Korea was an entirely different war, different rules. The rules had changed. Well, I went on to Korea, into

Vietnam. I had some close calls. But I still couldn't make the connection yet between the Creator and my experiences.

But in 1986, with this dream, it showed me many things. As a matter of fact, it was the 24th of May, about two o'clock in the morning, the usual time I woke up in the morning when I used to have nightmares. That's when the enemy would hit.

In this dream I was Sweating, all by myself as usual, as I have no one else who would join me except my brother who would show up once in a while unannounced . . . But this dream I had, I was by myself. And the stream that ran by the sweat lodge, I was in there bathing when the messenger spoke to me, and I couldn't see him. The voice kind of sounded familiar. It was something I had heard before, but I couldn't see who it was that told me: "Walk with me. I have some things to tell you."

We walked downstream, barefooted, no clothes on. This old man, this messenger, started telling me. He says, "You know who your people are. Your Elders have told you a long time ago, but most of the people have forgotten."

He named all of the people of the Salish Nation. He started from the North, and he started naming the Shuswap, the Lillooet, the Thompson, the Northern Okanagan, the Arrow Lakes, the Southern Okanagan, the Methow, the Chelan, the Nespelem, the Sanpoil, the Wenatchees, the Columbia, the Kalispel, the Pend d'Oreille, the Coeur d'Alene, and the Flatheads.

"Those are the people that speak the same language or similar as you. You have to remember that. Your language determines the boundaries of your territory."

He told me that I have much of the information already. All I have to do is put it to use . . . So I started thinking about that . . . As we walked, I'd jump across the creek once in a while. I'd jump across the creek because the path would narrow on one side of the creek . . . and finally, at one point, the old man had stopped talking. He hadn't said anything for a couple seconds. I jumped across the stream, and I ran into some stinging nettles, brushed my legs, and I started itching. I started scratching, and I woke up.

To make certain that I didn't forget, I got up; I lived out in the middle of the woods at the time, no electricity, so I lit a lamp and started writing down, taking notes of what had happened. Wrote down all the things that I was told. But before [I woke], he told me, "You have a purpose in this life, that's why you're here." He said, "Your grandfather told you."

And I tried to remember, "What did Grandfather tell me? What did he tell me?"

And I recalled the last time that I saw him before he died, I came up here to visit him . . . he lived right across the river here, and when I asked him after two weeks of storytelling—I listened to him day and night. I asked him finally, "Why are you telling me all these things?"

And he looked at me, and he sat there for a long time. He poured a drink of Pepsi, took a few sips and said, "Check your roots. The other thing I'm going to tell you is you're going to be standing toe to toe with the white government about our rights."

I kind of discounted that, forgot all about it.

About two years ago I was putting down the genealogy of hereditary Chiefs, and I kept seeing this name, Siwilixkin, while I was putting it in the computer. I kept seeing this name. It came up about two to three times. And I recalled it was his name, too. Then it dawned on me that I had a responsibility.

And although [my grandfather] had three given sons at the time that he could have passed this information on to, he chose me because the others were drinking, and he chose me and he gave me the responsibility as hereditary Chief, and that's when I realized what my real purpose was.

And for all my experiences, and for all the pain I've been through, after all these wars, I guess I used to curse the Creator for not letting me stay in his land. Then there are times I appreciate, then there are times I feel guilty for having survived when so many men have died, very good friends of mine, very good buddies—the people that I trusted that gave their lives so that I could live. I've had many guilts over that and I still do, I still carry that burden on my shoulder.

But now I know that I have done the things my grandfather told me that I'd be doing . . . And with all the experiences I've had all over the world and all of the cultures that I've experienced and watched and seen what has happened, I started to put all of that together, recapitulating all those experiences, and I find that now I'm fighting another kind of war in which the white man has taken—as in the words of Chief Dan George, "The white man has taken all of my weapons away; the only weapons I have left is the word."

I guess that's my battle now.

In this, the Okanagan, there has been young people who have been arming themselves to go to war, and I've had a hard time to convince, to persuade them, that once they've fired that first shot, that from that day on if they love to sleep, they'll never get another chance to get a full six or eight hours of sleep.

And if they keep coming to meetings late like they always have, they'll be late for their own funeral because they'll have been late for the battle . . .

They [the non-Natives] want our land. The only thing they have in common with us is they build their houses and villages on the land. We are part of the land; we are part of Mother Earth, just as the water, the forests, the mountains, the rocks, the Grandfather Sun, the Grandmother Moon; we are all part of this creation in that we, as the human people, when we were first created were designed to be the caretakers of Mother Earth. We are the ones . . .

Our major leaders in the past have been asked to define Aboriginal rights and they can't do it because they want to be so technical. But it's so simple; Aboriginal rights are the rights to survive. How do you survive? Food, clothing, water, shelter. That's it, in short—no more, no less. That's what I've been fighting for . . .

What I have to say, it's not what I know, it's what my Elders have taught me. I personally do not know these things, they're all teachings that have been passed on to me. I cannot take credit for any of this knowledge, the wisdom or the skills that I pass on. For I attribute these virtues through all of my Ancestors before me . . .

So with that I will conclude by stating in all of the things that have been passed onto me and I pass on to others, I hope that they keep an open mind. For the human mind is like a parachute; it must be opened before it can work. Thank you.

* * *

This interview is posted on my SoundCloud account. You can listen to Mr. Douglas share this story with me as I've converted the cassette tape to MP4 and uploaded it for the world to listen to (find the link in the Resources on page 189).

Glen's story for me matters so much because when I interviewed him, I had no idea he would welcome me into his life story in such an open way. I had no idea he'd share his miracle story with me. We need to tell the stories of our warriors and soldiers and veterans so that we can learn from them. Storytellers are teachers and they protect us by telling us what has come before and what may come again.

There are so many wonderful storytellers out there just waiting to share their truths with the right listeners so those listeners can become the storytellers of the future and carry the stories forward. Stories are meant to travel, and we honour our Elders and Knowledge Keepers when we share the stories we've been given in a good way. You are only stronger when you say, "I have permission to share this story," because, when you've observed protocol and given gifts and payment and you have permission to share an incredible story like Glen's, or Pauline's, or Anna's, or any of the storytellers I've shared here, please know they have all been paid and gifted. Contracts have also been signed to observe legal permission with my publisher. But, most importantly, I am indebted to each of the storytellers I've honoured here for life. I will continue to gift them and honour them and help them as much as I can.

It's the least I can do for the stories I've been blanketed with. My goodness, these stories have given me a faith and they have made my heart dance for decades now and will continue to do so.

And I hope they blanket you too. 😊

PROMPTS AND
HOW-TOs
TO GET YOU
GOING

28.
NOW GO FORTH, STORYTELLERS, AND PARTICIPATE!

We've been through quite a few of my techniques, a few of the reasons we need to tell stories, and a few of my favourite stories. Remember, it's up to you now to keep it going. If you still feel stuck or unsure, let me share this with you, one more bit of homework. Here's a game for you to help you get talking as you start to gather with people—even if it must be virtually! They are prompts to get an evening of storytelling going with your family, or a morning gathering with your classroom, or an intimate setting of friends. These are great for all ages, including kids.

GREAT PROMPTS FOR FAMILY GATHERINGS

1. My favourite memory of myself is the time
   ....

2. My favourite memory of you is
   ....

3. The medicine power I've inherited from our family is ...., and I can prove it with this story: ....

4. The medicine power I've inherited from my friends is ...., and here's a story of how this came to be:

....

5. My biggest wish for my family is that we ...., and here's why:

....

6. My biggest wish for your family is

....

7. The funniest thing that happened to me this year is the time ....

8. What I remember most from Dad or Mom or Aunty or Uncle is ...., and here's why: ....

9. One of the biggest gifts you've brought to my life is.., and here's why:

....

10. My first memory of you is ....

11. I can prove that the world is magic with this story:

....

12. I was given my name because ....

13. I adore you because ....

14. I want to be remembered for ....

15. The time I laughed so hard I cried was when

....

29.
HOW TO HOST A COMMUNITY STORYTELLING EVENT

Okay, maybe you don't feel quite ready. I've asked you to you to go forth and start gathering and sharing stories and help with the great Reclaiming for your family and community and for future generations.

It's okay to be nervous. They say if you're nervous it's because it matters to you. Let me share a story of one storytelling event that I hosted.

I was asked to host a community visiting event in High Level, Alberta, on May 15, 2016. It was to be for four hours—10:00 a.m. to 2:00 p.m.—at a lovely café called Traditions Garden Café and Gift Shop. This boutique has something for everyone: from Italian sodas, to high-end dresses, cool plaques for the cabin and garage, and flowers. The event was a complete success with around forty people coming and going. Some came in to grab a coffee and stayed with us for an hour or more; some stopped in for a muffin and a tea and had to run, but they enjoyed seeing so many community members sitting and chatting.

Here's what I brought to the party: the braille editions of our children's books, *A Man Called Raven* and *What's the Most Beautiful Thing You Know About Horses?* with George Littlechild (Lee and Low Books). I also brought copies of my first novel, *The Lesser Blessed*, signed by all of the actors and production team of the movie with First Generation Films (this was a complete hit!), copies of my graphic novels, *A Blanket of Butterflies* and *Three Feathers* (Portage and Main Press), my comics, *Path of the Warrior* and *Kiss Me Deadly* (The Healthy Aboriginal Network). I also brought a copy of the award-winning anthology that I'm in: *Moonshot* (AH Comics). The books were an invitation to touch and feel and read and see some of my greatest accomplishments. But they were also a gentle welcome into sitting down, having a drink, and enjoying a lovely afternoon with friends, neighbours, new friends, and a host (moi) who took time sharing stories that entertained. But I used all of this to "fish" for more stories.

Fishing is a technique where you start with a great story that welcomes everyone in and, hopefully, gets everyone going.

My opening was about being a writer-trainee for a month for the CBC hit television series *North of 60* back in the 90s. I was also a Cultural Consultant for the series for several seasons. Holy cow, it was fun. *North of 60* was filmed in Bragg Creek, Alberta and will always be one of Canada's most successful television shows with devoted fans. You can watch every episode for free with permission from the producers on YouTube. I was on set for one month as a writer-trainee. Seeing the actors, being a part of a production team, and helping to bring my northern influence to the scripts—it was life changing.

My suggestions for anyone wanting to host a community storytelling event are to:

- have it where people can buy their favourite drinks and light snacks;
- bring props that can be handed out and returned to you because those are storytelling prompts that can engage even the shyest guest. Bring gifts to give out. Bring something that you have all the passion in the world for: vintage Star Wars toys, porcupine quills that you harvested yourself for the purpose of craft making, traditional medicines, or rare Dinky Toys. There's nothing like being welcomed into another person's rapture. Passion is contagious. The best part of any interaction is walking away a little wiser and a little humbled by seeing someone so in love with life and their craft;
- have your event for a few hours. These days families are juggling sports, babysitters, work, meals, naps, etc. Chances are a lot of people want to come and listen and share—they just need more time to get there; and
- avoid using the time to sell. I purposely didn't want to sell any of my books. Why? I wanted to take that pressure out of the room. I wanted to be a guest with stories as gifts to share, not in business mode. With that tension gone, all I had to do was enjoy.

The event lasted four and a half hours. I had a smoothie, a chicken wrap, an Americano, and a glass of water. And I noticed a few things. While I was supposed to be the host, there were a few ladies to the left who were visiting in their corner of the three tables we had moved together. A few other business owners were talking about the next council meeting in the community. I got a few questions like, "When did you know you wanted to be a writer?" which I'm always so happy to answer. The key here is that after about two hours of visiting and sharing stories, our Circle took on a life of its own. When it would get quiet and there'd be new visitors at our table, I told another story about how we turned *The Lesser Blessed*, the novel, into a movie. It took seven years and $2.2 million (give or take), but we did it and it was all worth it. I shared stories about growing up in the North, which everyone at the table could relate to. Most of all, I do feel that everyone who joined us was honoured. I stood to shake hands every time someone came in to shake hands, and I stood to shake hands or receive a hug every time someone left. It was fun. It was soul warming. It was community building. Time flew—it was a fantastic event and one I'd be happy to take part in again.

If this is something you want in your community, please look at your community calendar. Is there something you'd like to honour? The return of the geese? The bears waking up? The full moon? Solstice? Remember, look at the calendar you've been creating! What is happening in the natural world to celebrate? Or what about a spiritual event that is celebrated? A sister event with another community? Have fun with this.

If you are lonesome for stories and friends, this storytelling celebration is a quick way to welcome abundance.

Mahsi cho to everyone who came out and mahsi cho to our hosts.

30.
PROTOCOL WHEN INVITING A VISITING ARTIST, ELDER, OR KNOWLEDGE KEEPER AS A GUEST TO YOUR SCHOOL*

This is a very important list, and I've marked its importance by placing it here as a final checklist. I know you'll get this right and you can do this with style and gusto! ☺

I use this list when I go to schools, but you can adapt it for any storytelling event!

1. Put up a big bright sign welcoming your Storyteller to your school on your website, in your school foyer, on your school announcement board, and in your morning and/or afternoon announcements. This lets parents, teachers, students, and visitors know that a special event is happening today.

....

*   *And It Can Be Adapted for when You Invite a Living Treasure to Your Organization*

2. Offer the storyteller a special parking spot close to your school entrance.

3. Greet your guest outside of your school with a smile and a handshake. Often, there are many locked doors outside of a school and no one wants to appear to be lost or trying to break into your school. Guest parking can be confusing with staff parking, student parking, etc. Keep an eye out for each other. We all want to be welcomed as a special guest.

4. Offer your storyteller tobacco and a gift from your school when you meet them as a sign of respect. A blanket is always lovely or a hoody with your school mascot. Tobacco shows respect. It shows you acknowledge them as an honoured guest. My Elder and Aunty Eileen Beaver is a mental health worker, an actor, an author, and a translator. She babysat me when I was thirteen months old. She and her husband, Henry Beaver, are the stars in our new movie *Three Feathers*. She shared this teaching about protocol with me: "Tobacco is a plant. It represents kindness, respect, honour, and wisdom. When you want to receive knowledge from Creation, you must ask in kindness and respect while asking for help. You approach with good intentions and acknowledge the help and gifts from the plant, elderly, any that is requested from Creation. One offers tobacco as a source of repaying for the request. If it is an emotional, physical, mental, or spiritual request to an Elder, do not expect an immediate response to be given. Sometimes an Elder can be silent for a while

as he or she prays on giving an answer to help or not. And sometimes a response of acceptance will be a swift yes or no. Tobacco is a sacred plant on the Medicine Wheel. It is used for offering thanks. One must give in order to request or receive knowledge as gifts. It is like money, but this tobacco must be given. If you are going into a Sweat, one offers tobacco and a cotton or broadcloth as well. It is up to you to later offer money to help for the pickers, Elders, and so on. The money is a part of appreciation for the help and not payment for the medicine knowledge. One might say if you pay very little, when you are very grateful, your respect and honour is of little value for the help. Therefore, honouring the gift of an Elder for your request greatly depends upon your heart."

5. When you gift the pouch of tobacco, you can say, "Thank you for sharing your knowledge with us today. The staff and students cannot wait to meet you and share time with you."

6. Wear a name tag so your storyteller will always remember who you are. Tell them the name of your school mascot. Are you "The Eagles," "The Cubs," or "The Pickles"? This is an easy way for anyone to greet each classroom or audience. It's also a fun surprise when students see that you have some inside information on who they are as a school community.

7. Offer them healthy food before they begin their work, as well as coffee, tea, or water.

Be sure they have water and/or a hot drink within reach while they are speaking.

8. Show them where the bathrooms are. Print up their schedules and have each teacher in the room introduce themselves as they walk in with a handshake.

9. Assign a student helper with a name tag if you can. Choose a student to check on them throughout the day. Does this visitor need art supplies or markers that work? Is your guest thirsty? Do they need photocopying done?

10. Make sure your guest has a hot and healthy lunch waiting for them during their break. This way they are not scrambling to find nourishment during the limited time for lunch. Food is fuel, food is comfort, and food is time to plan the good work ahead. Also have snacks ready to eat in case they've had a long drive in.

11. Give them the password to your WiFi. If your guest is working at your school all day, they'll be contacting their families and are probably juggling quite a few things.

12. Offer them tea, coffee, more snacks, and water throughout the day.

13. Send the schedule to your guest days in advance with your cell phone number so they can tell you if that works for them. Ten presentations in one day can be exhausting for anyone. It's no fun being surprised by a school schedule on the day of presentations. If your presenter has a schedule in advance, they can work with you to create a schedule that works for them and their presentation style.

14. Have a microphone in every room for them. A voice can only be projected for so long, and some some Elders, Knowledge Keepers, and visiting artists are hearing-impaired.

15. Give your guest breaks and show them where they can leave their jackets in a secure environment so they do not have to carry them into every room. Breaks are important for health reasons. Some guests have to take medications at carefully prescribed times throughout the day.

16. Please ask your guests what kind of honorarium they prefer and what payment method works for them well before the event. At the end of the day, have their payment ready. Offer a thank you card, a gift of thank you, and give a speech honouring them for sharing their time, their talents, and their inspiration. Some Elders prefer cash as they are on a limited income.

17. Invite them back if it's a great fit. There's nothing like knowing a favourite mentor is coming back to visit your school again.

18. Tell your instructors that they are still "on" when a guest is presenting to the class. Sometimes when guests present, instructors use this time to prepare upcoming work or mark assignments. If the class starts to get rowdy, the presenter can become distracted. We are all there to learn together. Be sure that your classroom is prepared and organized to treat the guest and the listeners in the most respectful of ways. Students deserve to know that when a living treasure has chosen

to share what they know with them, this
is a high honour for everyone. Treat this
opportunity to learn with great respect as you
will have these stories and these teachings for
the rest of your life.

Artists, Elders, Knowledge Keepers, and guests can
show students and teachers and administrators something they may have never considered: these people
may become mentors and friends that you can count
on in the future. Have fun!

Mahsi cho.

AFTERWORDS

31.
SIX POUNDS

recently had the pleasure of going for my annual checkup. We have a great family doctor here in Edmonton. To my surprise she told me that I was overweight. Me? I thought I was still in my prime: 165 pounds. That's what I was in high school!

Well, at the tender age of forty-six, I was six pounds over what a six-foot one man should weigh.

That's right, Cousins. My Elders were right: Old Richy Van Camp has been packing in the pounds all these blessed years.

I was demolished.

My doctor could tell.

"Okay, Richard," she said. "Here's what you're going to do. Every night, you're going to leave your cell phone at home, and you're going to take that gorgeous wife of yours and that beautiful son of yours and you're going to go for a walk, and you're going to talk, and you're going to connect, and those pounds are going to melt right off. I promise. And, best of all, think of what you'll truly gain as husband and wife, as parents, as friends, as a family."

So, my friends, I share this with you in hopes that you do the same with your sweetie, your children, your family, your friends, your pets, and everything around you—that you spend time and connect. Time shared, laughter, a safe home, a heart-to-heart hug, cherished memories, health, family, friends, great food, a good book, community radio, a lovely TV series, a movie that swoons you, adventures and milestones—personal and as a family—this is what life is all about. I think perhaps it took the pandemic to remind us all of that. Every day is precious. Enjoy today.

32.
WRAPPING UP IN A GOOD WAY, BETTER THAN WE FOUND EACH OTHER

My wish for you is that you surround yourself with the sweet medicine of the world and become a storyteller that your friends and family admire.

May you always have enough to share.

May you continuously have to shop for Tupperware because most of your absolute best cooking has gone home with family and friends who never wanted your sweet visits to end.

May you know precious things that the world is forgetting. May you share and practice them to honour them.

May you hear stories weekly that make your soul hum.

May your days be meaningful and filled with purpose and great food.

May you be a cherished neighbour who brightens your community. COVID taught us how very important these people are.

And, if I didn't say this before, mahsi cho for sharing time with me and the storytellers I adore.

Let's honour the upcoming years together by sharing great food, soul-nourishing stories, and watching our families grow to their full potential.

May the stars twinkle above during the summer months and the snow dance outside your home if you live where there is snow. And may you remember to share stories that protect the natural world so that even Mother Earth smiles.

And may the people and stories that connect us all continue.

Bring that love. Don't you ever stop.

And please don't wait to record your Elders—*with* permissions!—and family with audio and video recordings. Don't wait to give your loved ones their inheritances, their culture. Don't wait to bring your love or show it. Don't wait to say, "I love you," or "I'm sorry," or "I forgive you."

Don't wait to live.

Don't wait to love.

Don't wait to gather in a good way and share your stories.

***

Now you've read the stories of Tomson Highway, Maria Brown, Rosa Mantla, my mom Rosa Wah-Shee, Trevor Evans, Jace DeCory, Anna Tonasket, Pauline and Barrie Clarke, and Glen Douglas. And so now that you have the teaching of tobacco and the insights and wisdom of our community calendar and reclaimed star knowledge and now that you have all the tips, the protocols, and gentle nudges to get out there and start recording your Elders and family members, now you have more medicine than when we first met.

We're living the teaching of the great Bernie Berg-man, "Leave each place and each person better than you found them," because you have this teaching and these stories now. Share them. Travel them forward.

There is magic in the world and you are a part of it. Any time you share a story or a teaching, a joke or a laugh, or a great memory, you're adding to the beauty of the universe. I believe stories keep you healthy. They guide you. They remind you about what's most important in life, just like what Bernie Bergman told me a long time ago when I was a young man. Let's all continue to leave each person and each place better than we found them.

Mahsi cho and with great respect,
Richard Van Camp

THANK YOU

I am indebted to Nickita Longman, Karen Clark, and Bruce Walsh for inviting me to contribute to this series.

Gather is a life's work for me. I have dedicated my life to being a caretaker of stories that nourish my soul. I do this for myself, for my family, for my community, and for anyone needing the good nourishing medicine that comes from a great story and a great visit that can bring hope and peace and comfort.

I really want to thank Karen Clark, Kelly Laycock, and Rhonda Kronyk for editing this manuscript. It's one thing to spend decades collecting stories and craft; it's another to put it into a binding narrative that flows. Please know that any mistakes in this manuscript are my own, and we'll do our best to correct them if we learn of any mistakes.

I am grateful to University of Regina Press because *Gather* is a dream come true for me. I hope you love this book as much as I do and return to it as many times as you need to for sweet soul medicine and inspiration. If you have questions, reach out to me on Facebook or Twitter or through my website: www.richardvancamp.com.

The great news about the time we live in is I've uploaded the audio files of Glen Douglas and Maria Brown sharing their stories about visiting Heaven on my SoundCloud account.* I've also added Anna Tonasket's story about being saved by the Little People. Just google "Richard Van Camp" and "SoundCloud" and you'll hear them. There's also a pile of other great recordings and interviews and readings. Enjoy.

Also, I started a YouTube channel to upload my stories and interviews. You'll see me retell the late and great Trevor Evans's story about the moose and the Pipe. Enjoy. There's a pile of other videos on there that I hope give you the giggles.

Who are my favourite storytellers? Ivan Coyote, Ivy Chelsea, Solomon Ratt, Henry and Eileen Beaver, Earl Evans, Kenny Hudson, Richard Mercredi, Sr., my mom Rosa, my uncle Alex Washie, the late Trevor Evans, Norma Gauthier, Rose Richardson, and everyone I've included in this book. There are so many more generous souls who I admire, but here's a great start to what I hope we can all build on: the return of storytelling, the

---

* For the Joe Mabillon that Maria Brown sees in her visit to Heaven, you can hear in the unclear audio on Sound-Cloud that she names him several times. Joe Mabillon was Maria's neighbour when they were both alive, so I'm going on this information in the transcription. If I'm wrong, I take full responsibility.

return of visiting, and the return of lifting each other up when we need it most.

And I am grateful to you for sharing time with me and the storytellers and Knowledge Keepers that I admire.

Here's to the return of community and to the return to the best of ourselves together.

In friendship and with respect,
Richard Van Camp

ACKNOWLEDGEMENTS

An earlier version of "Cheat Sheet! A.K.A. Uncle Richard's Storytelling Tips" was published by Douglas & McIntyre in *Me Artsy*. Thank you to the publisher for permission to adapt and reprint it here.

I would like to acknowledge with everything inside of me the generous funds awarded to me by the Blue Metropolis International Literary Festival. Their monetary award given to me for receiving the Blue Metropolis First Peoples Literary Prize allowed me to repay the storytellers and Knowledge Keepers in *Gather*. I am so grateful to the Festival and humbled and honoured by this award. Mahsi cho. Thank you very much!

RESOURCES

Here are more resources for you to read and consult as you continue your journey.

SoundCloud Recordings

> Maria Brown: https://soundcloud.com/richardvan-camp/mariah-brown-side-b-1-2
>
> Glen Douglas: https://soundcloud.com/richard-vancamp/okanagan-elder-and-war-veteran-glen-douglas-shares-a-miracle-story-with-me
>
> Anna Tonasket: https://soundcloud.com/richard-vancamp/anna-tonasket-and-how-the-little-peo-ple-saved-my-life

Other Books by Richard Van Camp

Novels

> *The Lesser Blessed*. Douglas & McIntyre, 1996.
> *Whistle*. Pearson Canada, 2015.

Novella

When We Play Our Drums, They Sing! McKellar &
Martin, 2018 (flip book with Monique Gray
Smith's *Lucy & Lola*).

Short Story Collections

Angel Wing Splash Pattern. Kegedonce Press, 2002.
Godless but Loyal to Heaven. Enfield & Wizenty, 2013.
The Moon of Letting Go. Enfield & Wizenty, 2010.
Night Moves. Enfield & Wizenty, 2015.
Moccasin Square Gardens. Douglas & McIntyre, 2019.

Children's Books

A Man Called Raven. Lee & Low Books, 1997.
What's the Most Beautiful Thing You Know About Horses?
Children's Book Press, 2003.
Welcome Song for Baby. Orca Book Publishers, 2007.
Nighty Night. McKellar & Martin, 2012.
Little You. Orca Book Publishers, 2013.
We Sang You Home. Orca Book Publishers, 2016.
Kiss by Kiss. Orca Book Publishers, 2018.
May We Have Enough to Share. Orca Book Publishers,
2019.

Graphic Novels

Path of the Warrior. Healthy Aboriginal Network,
2010.
Kiss Me Deadly. Healthy Aboriginal Network, 2011.
Three Feathers. Portage & Main Press, 2015.
A Blanket of Butterflies. Portage & Main Press, 2015.
The Blue Raven. Pearson Canada, 2015.
Spirit. South Slave Divisional Education Council,
2015.

Tributes

> *Our Stories Help The Northern Lights Dance*
> *Solus: Kent Williams*

Recommended Books and Resources on the Craft of Storytelling

Archibald, Jo-Ann. *Indigenous Storywork: Educating the Heart, Mind, Body, and Spirit.* Vancouver: UBC Press, 2008.

Armstrong, Helen. "Indigenizing the Curriculum: The Importance of Story." *First Nations Perspectives* 5, no. 1 (2013): 37–64. events.ufv.ca/tlc/wp-content/uploads/sites/8/2014/10/Indigenizing-the-Curriculum-The-Importance-of-Story-1.pdf.

Attwood, Bain and Fiona Magowan, eds. *Telling Stories: Indigenous History and Memory in Australia and New Zealand.* London: Allen & Unwin, 2002.

Blondin, George. *Trail of the Spirit: Mysteries of Medicine Power Revealed.* Edmonton: NeWest Press, 2006.

———. *Yamoria the Lawmaker.* Edmonton: NeWest Press, 1997.

———. *When the World Was New: Stories of the Sahtú Dene.* Yellowknife: Outcrop, the Northern Publishers, 1990.

Cortes, Victoria Roca. "Oral Storytelling as a Pedagogical and Learning Tool for Cultural and Cross-Cultural Understanding." *Master of Teaching Research Projects*, University of Toronto, ON, May 2016. http://hdl.handle.net/1807/72174.

Helm, June. *Power and Prophecy Among the Dogrib Indians.* Lincoln: University of Nebraska Press, 1994.

Hulan, Renee and Renate Eigenbrod, eds. *Aboriginal Oral Traditions: Theory, Practice, Ethics.* Halifax, NS: Fernwood Publishing, 2008.

King, Thomas. *The Truth about Stories: A Native Narrative.* Minneapolis: University of Minnesota Press, 2008.

MacLean, Melanie and Linda Wason-Ellam. "When Aboriginal and Métis Teachers Use Storytelling as an Instructional Practice." A grant report to the Aboriginal Education Research Network, Saskatchewan Learning, 2006. https:// documents.sd61.bc.ca/ANED/educational-Resources/Storytelling/Storytelling_As_An_ Instructional_Practice.pdf

Martin, Keavy. *Stories in a New Skin: Approaches to Inuit Literature.* Winnipeg: University of Manitoba Press, 2012.

McCall, Sophie. *First Person Plural: Aboriginal Storytelling and the Ethics of Collaborative Authorship.* Vancouver: UBC Press, 2011.

Napoleon, Art, ed. *Bushland Spirit: Our Elders Speak.* Moberly Lake, BC: Twin Sister Publishing, 1988.

Palmer, Jr., Gus. *Telling Stories the Kiowa Way.* Tucson: University of Arizona Press, 2003.

Roberston, David A. and Julie Flett. *When We Were Alone.* Winnipeg: Highwater Press, 2016.

Robinson, Eden. *The Sasquatch at Home: Traditional Protocols and Modern Storytelling.* Edmonton: University of Alberta Press, 2011.

Sheftel, Anna and Stacey Zembrzycki. *Oral History Off the Record: Toward an Ethnography of Practice.* New York: Palgrace MacMillan, 2013.

Simpson, Leanne Betasamosake. *Dancing on Our Turtle's Back: Stories of Nishnaabeg Re-Creation, Resurgence, and a New Emergence.* Winnipeg: ARP Books, 2011.

Smith, Monique Gray. *Speaking Our Truth: A Journey of Reconciliation.* Victoria, BC: Orca Book Publishers, 2017.

Yakeleya, Elizabeth, Sarah Simon, and other Sahtú and Gwich'in Elders. *We Remember the Coming of the White Man.* Edited by Sarah Stewart; Foreword, Raymond Yakeleya; Afterword, Colette Poitras. Calgary: Durvile and Uproute Books, 2020.

Handbooks, Manuals, and Guides

Maynes, Mary Jo. *Telling Stories: The Use of Personal Narratives in the Social Sciences and History.* Ithaca, NY: Cornell University Press, 2008.

Ritchie, Donald A. *Doing Oral History: A Practical Guide.* Oxford: Oxford University Press, 2003.

Trimble, Charles E., Barbara W. Sommer, and Mary Kay Quinlan. *The American Indian Oral History Manual: Making Many Voices Heard.* Walnut Creek, CA: Left Coast Press, 2008.

Yow, Valerie Raleigh. *Recording Oral History: A Guide for the Humanities and Social Sciences.* Lanham, MD: Rowman & Littlefield, 2015.

Resources on Indigenous Storytelling in Practice

In overcoming trauma

Cave, Mark and Stephen M. Sloan. *Listening on the Edge: Oral History in the Aftermath of Crisis.* Oxford: Oxford University Press, 2014 (collection of interviews; international scope).

Linklater, Renee. *Decolonizing Trauma Work: Indigenous Stories and Strategies*. Halifax, NS: Fernwood Publishing, 2014 (theory and case studies).

Storytelling as resistance

Emberley, Julia. *The Testimonial Uncanny: Indigenous Storytelling, Knowledge, and Reparative Practices.* New York: SUNY Press, 2002.

Oral history in law

Miller, Bruce Granville. *Oral History on Trial: Recognizing Aboriginal Narratives in the Courts.* Vancouver: UBC Press, 2011.

Business and self-help books on storytelling

Biesenbach, Rob. *Unleash the Power of Storytelling: Win Hearts, Change Minds, Get Results.* Eastlawn Media, 2018.

Choy, Esther K. *Let the Story Do the Work: The Art of Storytelling for Business Success.* AMACOM, 2017.

Dicks, Matthew. *Storytelling: Engage, Teach, Persuade, and Change Your Life through the Power of Storytelling.* New World Library, 2018.

Simmons, Annette. *The Story Factor: Inspiration, Influence, and Persuasion through the Art of Storytelling.* Basic Books, 2006.

RICHARD VAN CAMP is a proud Tłįchǫ Dene from Fort Smith, NWT, and the author of over twenty-four books, including the Eisner-nominated graphic novel *A Blanket of Butterflies*. His bestselling novel, *The Lesser Blessed*, has been made into a movie that has received critical acclaim. He lives in Edmonton, Alberta. You can visit Richard on Facebook, Twitter, and and YouTube, and at www.richardvancamp.com.